hotshops

Author: Arian Mostaedi
Publishers: Carles Broto & Josep Mª Minguet
Architectural Adviser: Pilar Chueca
Editorial Coordination: Jacobo Krauel & Joan Fontbernat
Graphic Design & Production: Héctor Navarro
Layout: Federico Orozco
Text: Contributed by the architects,
edited by Jacobo Krauel
Cover photograph: © Alberto Piovano

© Links International
Jonqueres, 10. 1-5. 08003 Barcelona, Spain
Tel.: +34 93 301 21 99 · Fax: +34 93 301 00 21
info@linksbooks.net · www.linksbooks.net

Edition 2004

Printed in Barcelona, Spain

hotshops

introduction

The standard for commercial spaces has undergone dramatic changes in recent years, due in large part to the rapid growth of shopping centers and an outcropping of new shops which have to fight for a foothold amidst fierce competition.

The proliferation of these new businesses has engendered different ways of viewing the layout of the sales floor, the experimentation with light and color as architectural resources in and of themselves, the use of pre-fabricated materials and a widespread tendency toward the creation of diaphanous spaces with the bare minimum of divisions.

In compiling the most representative guide possible to current and future trends in shop design, we have included a diverse sampling of spaces, with their seemingly endless possibilities in layout and interior design.

Furthermore, in an effort to provide much more than a comprehensive overview of each project, we have also included the most characteristic details of the construction process, which is often an essential part of the work's character. Each project includes a wide variety of floor plans, sketches and construction details, as well as a description of the work as conceived by the architect.

- **John Pawson** · Jigsaw — 8
- **eok: eichinger oder knechtl** · Laks-Watch — 18
- **Antonio Citterio** · Mariella Burani / Vivere — 28
- **Javier Maroto & Alvaro Soto** · La Oreja de Plata II — 36
- **Rei Kawakumbo** · Comme des Garçons — 46
- **J. Grego & J. Smolenicky** · Zelo Hairdresser — 58
- **David Chipperfield** · Joseph Menswear — 66
- **Marta de Rezio** · Kickers — 76
- **Roger Hirsch** · IS Industries Stationery Store — 84
- **Claudio Silvestrin** · Giorgio Armani Store — 92
- **Eric Raffy** · Cabin Racing Team — 100
- **Claudio Silvestrin** · Starkmann's Office / Johan Menswear Shop — 106
- **Lazzarini Pickering Architetti** · Fendi Boutique — 114
- **I. Vilela, J. Armas & R. Ruano** · Farmacia Tenoya — 124
- **Michael Gabellini** · Boutique Jil Sander — 130
- **Patrick Genard** · Sephora — 138

- **Studio Baciocchi** · Miu Miu — 148
- **Pepa Poch** · Peluquerías Salva G — 158
- **Claudio Nardi** · Ferre' Jeans Boutique — 168
- **Ramon Esteve** · Farrutx Palma — 176
- **Peter Marino Assoc. Architects** · Giorgio Armani — 184
- **Claudio Nardi** · Dolce & Gabbana / D&G — 192
- **Studio Cerri & Associati** · Boutique Salvini — 200
- **Creneau International Design** · Pepe Jeans — 210
- **Urquijo & Vázquez** · Purificación García — 220
- **Venturi, Scott Brown & Associates** · Exxon Gas Station for Disney World — 230
- **Jean Nouvel** · Galeries Lafayette / Euralille Centre Comercial — 238
- **Sage Wimmer Coombe** · Jancovic Plaza — 248
- **Vincent van Duysen** · Boutique Natan — 252
- **Frank F. Drewes** · Sally & Sam — 262
- **Javier Mozas** · Chemist's in calle Postas — 270
- **Peter Marino Assoc. Architects** · Louis Vuitton — 280

John Pawson
Jigsaw
London, UK

The basis for the design was the need for an appropriate platform to show Jigsaw's clothes off to their best advantage. The scheme invites, rather than intimidates customers, making them feel comfortable and welcome; nonetheless, it still projects a distinctive personality for the store. The existing frontage has been stripped away, with the twin apertures now framed in simple Portland stone panels.

Inside this semitransparent facade the first floor has been cut back to create a double height space, six meters high, establishing a sense of space and light for the shop while providing an area for display mannequins showing what the store has to offer.

What was once an irregular, rambling plan has been remodelled to give a sense of order and clarity. To this end a pair of staircases are positioned against one wall descending down to the lower level, making a virtue out of its non-orthogonal geometry. They are proportioned generously enough to make it immediately clear from the street that there is a second, equally important sales floor at the lower level. On the other side is a second staircase providing access for visitors to the pressroom above. The ground floor is planned around four distinct display areas set between a long low shelving unit that stretches back into the shop along the line of the staircase. Each area is defined by full-height, hand-etched acrylic screens that provide a sense of enclosure, minimising the visual impact of the necessary structural column. The cash and wrap area is positioned toward the rear of the store, screening the naturally illuminated changing area at the back. A similar strategy is used for the lower sales floor. Access from the upper level will be by way of a pair of staircases ranged along one wall and bringing customers into the centre of the lower floor. Changing rooms will be at the front, screened by etched acrylic panels, with cash and wrap at the back.

Photographs: Richard Glover

From outside, the shop gives an inviting appearance of order and clarity. The existing shopfront has been removed and the openings have been framed with simple portland cement panels. A pair of staircases aligned along the outer wall descend to the ground floor and are powerful visual features.

With its white walls and granite floor extending along the depth of the shop, the scheme gives a sense of space and proportion that underlines its originality.

The engraved acrylic glass panels divide the space and minimize the visual impact of the structural columns.

eok: eichinger oder knechtl
Laks-Watch
Vienna, Austria

A flagship store is developed as a prototype of a chain to be used worldwide. The concept therefore uses single, clearly differentiated and reproducible measurements that guarantee a recognisable style even when used in limited dimensions.

At the entrance a light element hangs in front of the facade for indirect flood lighting, with silver metal panels for a suction effect. The display cabinets have been replaced by flat interactive screens (equipped with microphones and speakers) with web pages sent from the head office of the firm.

A wide, inviting staircase leads down into the space from the entrance. All the display cabinets and sales modules are aligned along the wall and are not interrupted by the staircase. Even the cash desks and the general storage area are against the wall.

The module is made out of transparent Plexiglas with rear lighting. Customers can try on the watches which are hanging from steel cables with counterweights. The counter module is fitted with computer cash registers, packaging dispensers, etc. Nets with printed images and texts are stretched across the space. A yacht floor copes elegantly with the slopes of the ramps, and the ceiling is in white leather.

The light changes with the time of day. All wall lamps and spotlighting are adjustable; a control panel can call up different atmospheres.

All doors, extensions and cash registers play different, specially created melodies and noises when they are opened.

A room perfume created specially for the shop is distributed through the air conditioning system. All furniture and cash modules are organised according to a sales ritual that gives the staff confidence in their work. All module doors are secured with electronic locks that can be opened with the salesperson's wristwatch.

Photographs: Margherita Spiluttini

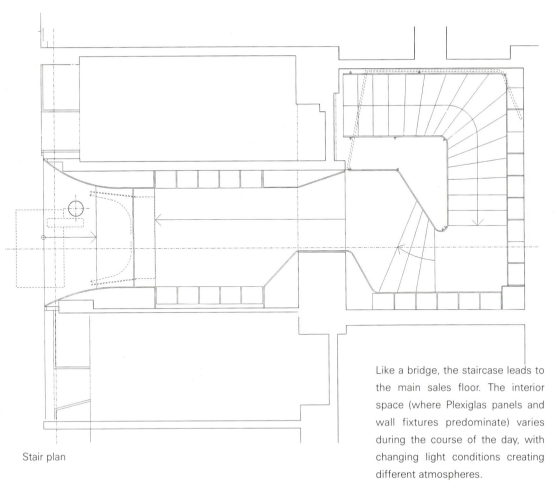

Stair plan

Like a bridge, the staircase leads to the main sales floor. The interior space (where Plexiglas panels and wall fixtures predominate) varies during the course of the day, with changing light conditions creating different atmospheres.

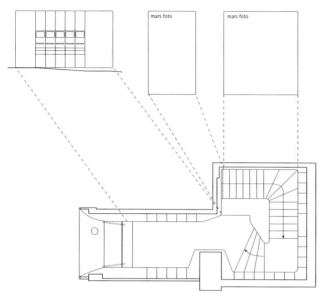

Stair floor plan

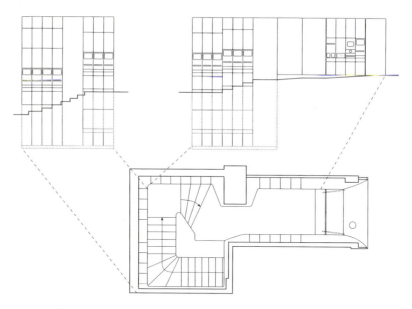

Stair floor plan

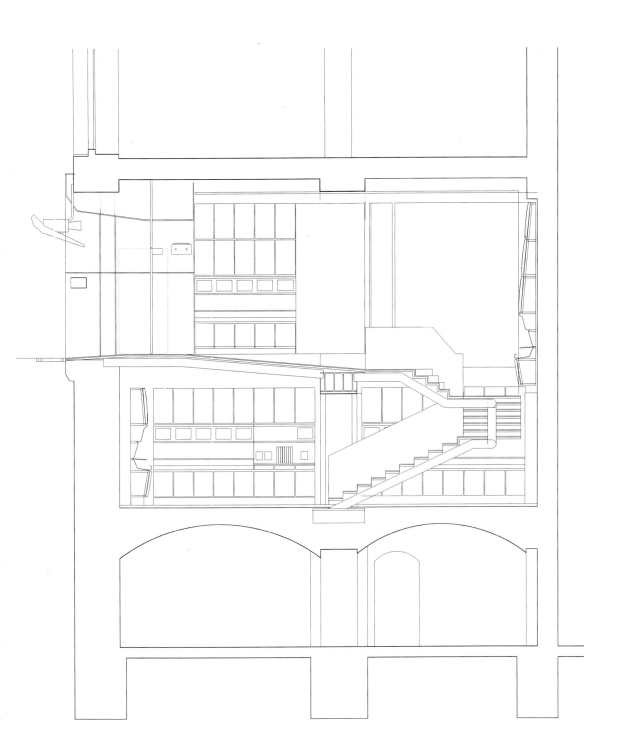

Cross section

The wood floor, Plexiglas panels and indirect lighting which illuminates reproductions of famous paintings highlight the watches displayed on counterweighted cables as if they were precious jewels.

Access section

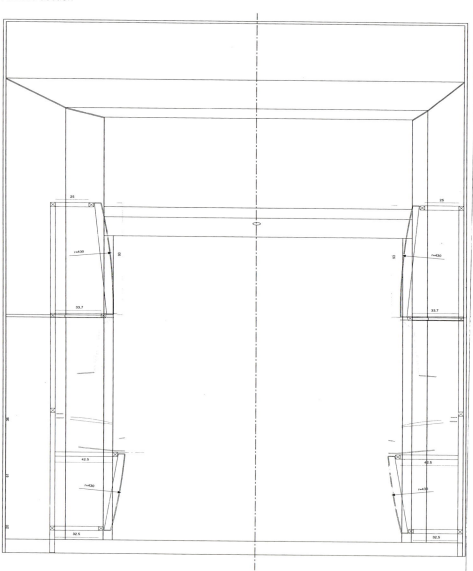

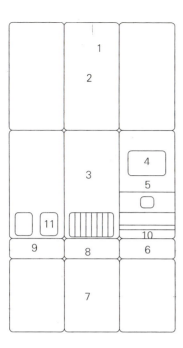
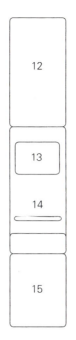

1. Doors
2. Packaging
3. Packaging
4. Screen
5. Scanner
6. Counter
7. Bags
8. Documents
9. Dispatch
10. Keyboard
11. Printer
12. Doors
13. Light panel
14. Tray
15. Watches

Counter elevation

Display unit elevation

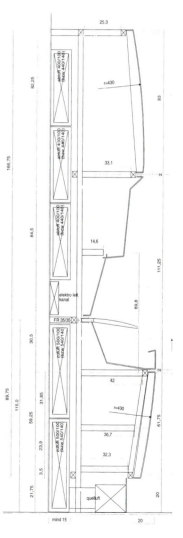

Display unit section

Antonio Citterio
Mariella Burani / Vivere
Milano, Italy

The Vivere and Mariella Burani boutiques, both in Milan, are schemes designed by the studio of Antonio Citterio. The former, located near the Duomo, is a space of 753 sq m spreading over three floors, while the latter occupies 100 sq m of the fashionable Milanese avenue *par excellence*, Via Montenapoleone. While these are very different projects, they do share a common idea, that of translating the philosophy of each respective company into architectural language.

This building, originally designed by Asnago and Vender in 1960, accommodates the Vivere furniture shop. The façade, with an aluminium and glass enclosure, towers above the street and leaves the shop interior open to passers-by. A staircase connects the three floors —basement, ground floor and first floor— without calling too much attention to the sensation of verticality. Shop fixtures are in walnut wood; paving, walls and staircase are white. Special note should be taken of the flooring, which is resin, a "secondary" material: the idea was to clear the setting of all relevance in order to create a museum-like feel in this exhibition space where the items on display predominate. Lighting is achieved through built-in ceiling lights. The idea behind the design of the Mariella Burani boutique denotes a strong link to nature and a search for simplicity. The interior spaces therefore form an interplay of simple and natural materials: white walls and ceiling, cherry wood flooring and fixtures and steel hangers. Access to the sales floor is gained through a glass door and a wooden ramp to the side. The sales floor itself is located one floor above street level and is arranged around a sitting area, which features a table and sofa designed by Citterio. The shelves and hangers are organised along the perimeters, where they are attached to the walls. A handful of built-in ceiling lamps light the space.

Photographs: Gionata Xerra

Mariella Burani

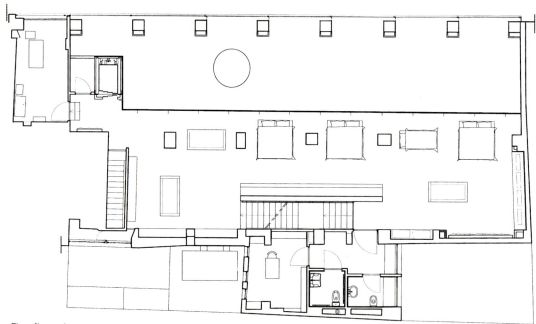

First floor plan

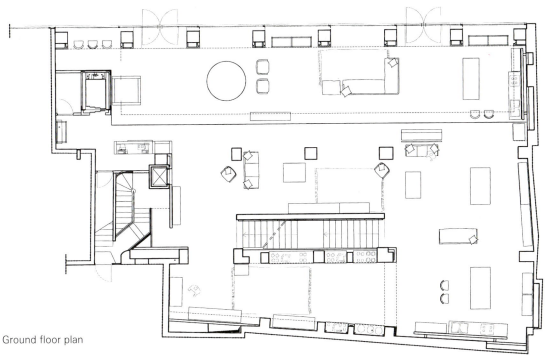

Ground floor plan

A circular well opens in the top two floors and communicates the three floors of the shop visually. The facade is solved with a transparent glass wall.

Vivere

Ground floor plan

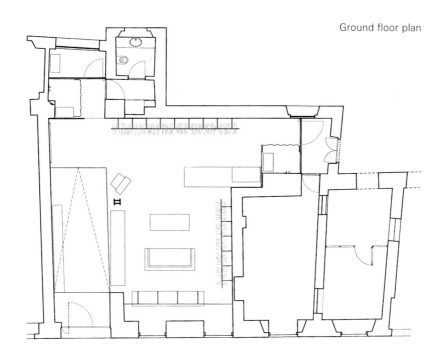

Citterio has created a delicate space in this Milan boutique of the firm Mariella Burani. The sobriety characteristic of his work is seen here in an environment inhabited by sparse furniture made in warm materials, and in the chromatic interplay of the white walls and the warm wooden floors.

Javier Maroto & Alvaro Soto
La Oreja de Plata II
Madrid, Spain

The jeweler's shop La Oreja de Plata II, for the designer Chus Burés, has two floors. The access floor from Calle Jorge Juan was previously only 7 sqm, with a lower space of approximately 40 sqm. The architects decided to make the entrance floor a void from which one descends a very transparent staircase, allowing the whole space to be perceived slowly. In fact, the architects imagined that the whole entrance would be felt from inside a shop window that customers would not leave until they had gone down to the lower floor. In this movement the visitors are accompanied by display cabinets and glass boxes suspended from the ceiling onto which light is projected. The jewels and the objects are thus exposed to view, casting evocative shades on the glass supports.

On the lower floor we find a rectangular room ("a Mediterranean space", as Chus Burés called it) that is gently lit from the top. The floor is of dark wooden planks without a skirting board that creaks under the feet of the customers.

The architects have constructed a radical and completely enclosed space, as most of the work was done in the basement. They were interested in the idea of projecting the variable brightness of the sunlight and the light that goes through each cabinet, thereby converting the small access at street level into a skylight which illuminates the lower level of the shop and contains an almost transparent staircase.

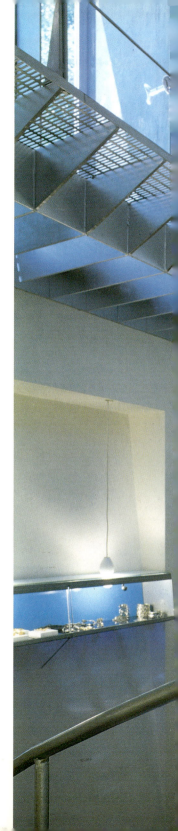

Photographs: Juan Merinero

The access to the shop is through a small space that acts as a shop window. The boundaries between the shop window and the staircases leading to the basement are blurred, creating a bright space in which the elements on display float freely.

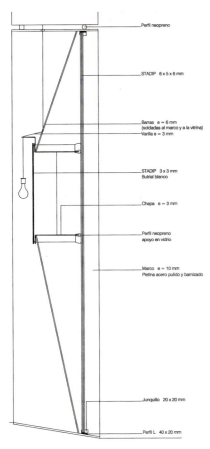

Section of the display cabinet
of the shop window

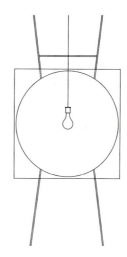

Section of a suspended cabinet

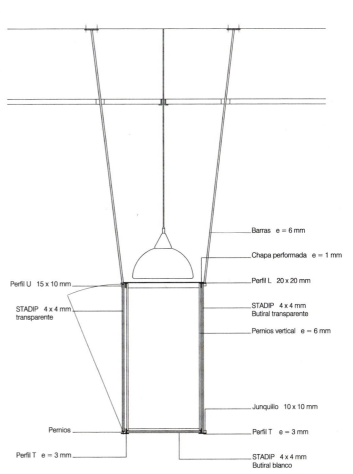

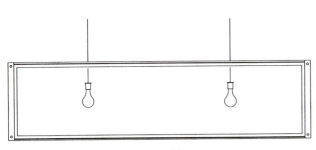

Elevation of a back-lit suspended cabinet

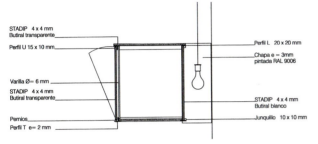

Section of a back-lit suspended cabinet

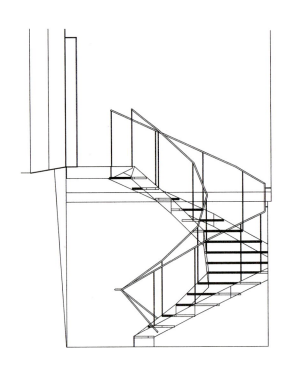

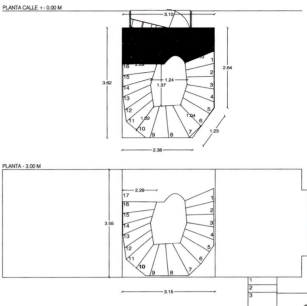

Stair plan

The artificial lighting is projected through the cabinets, transforming them into the lamps of the shop. They are variable in shape, location and brightness.

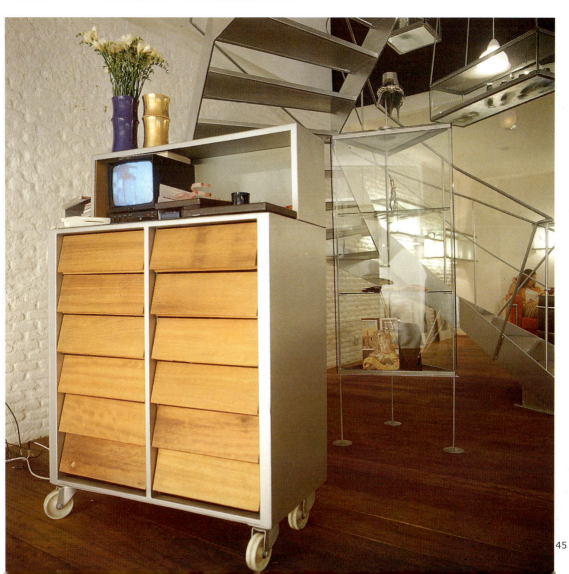

Rei Kawakumbo
Comme des Garçons
New York City, USA / Tokyo, Japan

The two new boutiques of Comme des Garçons in New York and Tokyo propose a new concept of commercial space: instead of purified atmospheres and minimalist facilities, complicity between the designer and the customers, and interaction between the person and the space are sought.

The headquarters of Comme des Garçons in New York has moved to the district of Chelsea. This new location responds to the unique characteristics of the boutique: it is a windowless building with an external brick skin and fire exit. Except for the mouth of the tunnel with its unusual red lights and white flooring, nothing reveals the presence of a space like Comme des Garçons. The tunnel is the element that defines the space and summarises its conceptual design: the idea is to achieve a feeling of expectation that leads to the active participation of the customers. This aluminium tunnel with a monocoque structure does not require ribs or braces. The lights set flush with the floor guide the visitor to the interior of the space. A swinging glass door marks the entrance to the enclosure, and a blind protects the entrance at night.

For the Aoyama shop, in Tokyo, the facade was renewed with walls of corrugated glass covered by a blue screen that isolates the shop and increases the curiosity of potential customers. The interior door leads to a space impregnated with the architect's personality. The idea that the client should not come into contact with the clothes immediately is predominant, so the space has been distributed in such a way that the garments are not immediately visible. The field of vision is blocked by large irregular structures of white-painted steel. According to Kawakubo, hiding the clothes means that the customers have to look for them themselves, in their own time. An atmosphere of tension is thus created. The corridors run through a succession of curved walls that lead to different spaces. Each of the spaces, decorated by the artists Christian Astugueivieille and Sophie Smallhorn, is conceived as a work of art that reproduces a different atmosphere and product.

Photographs: Masayuki Hayashi, Todd Eberle

New York City

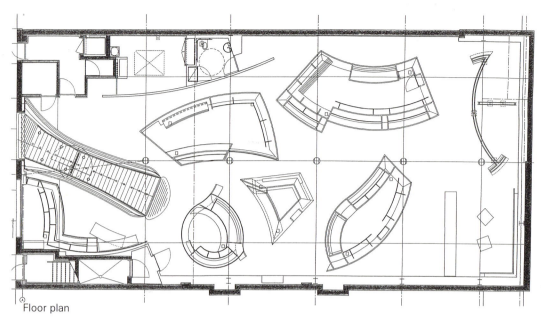

Floor plan

The boutique, resulting from the collaboration between Kawakubo and the Japanese architect Takao Kawasaki, is developed toward the interior like a labyrinth, with the tunnel as an entrance. Once inside the shop it is not possible to view the whole space, so the visitor must walk around it.

Tokyo

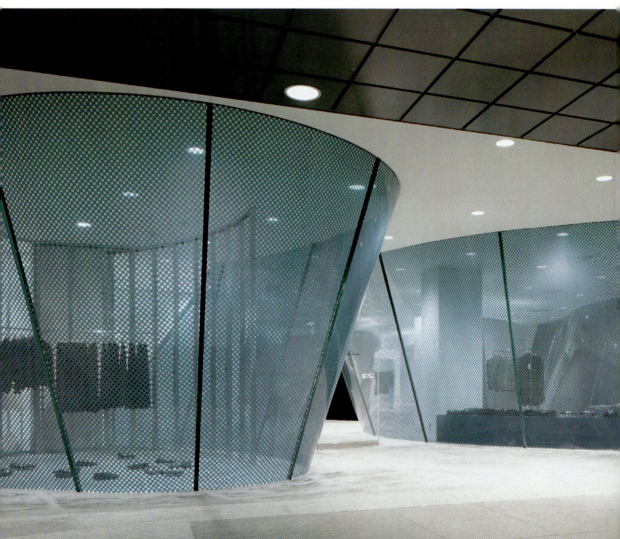

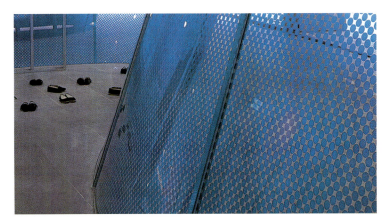

The new facade of corrugated glass covered by a dotted blue screen was designed by Future Systems of London. Although passers-by can see some of the clothes through the screen, privacy is a major feature of the interior.

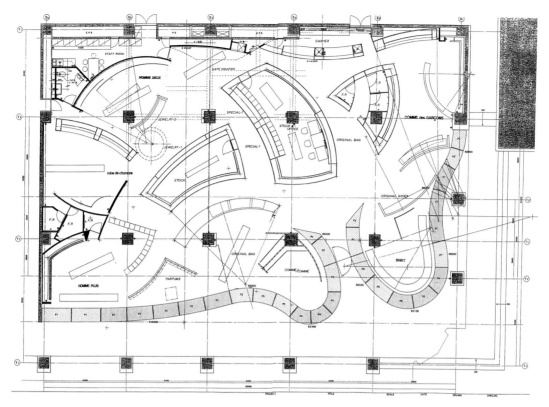

Floor plan

The varied treatment of the walls distinguishes the different exhibition spaces. Christian Astuguevieille and Sophie Smallhorn designed two of these spaces and Kawakubo designed the rest.

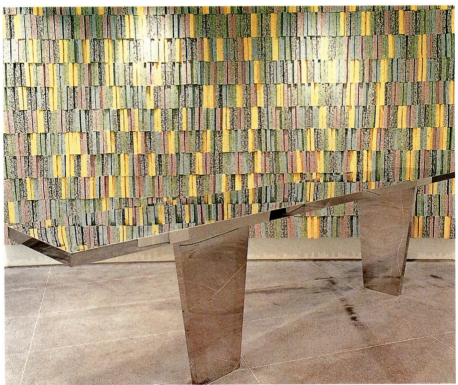

J. Grego & J. Smolenicky
Zelo Hairdresser
Zurich, Switzerland

A vibrantly coloured interior glows from behind a mellow grey sandstone facade. This relationship of colours between town and shop is a central element in the design. Visual charm, and the effect of advertising which is linked with it, is the real essence of the project. Its colourfulness is intended to achieve an effect which is similar to that of the enormous illuminated hoardings which cast a spell over the town at night.

In this instance, however, the advertising has not been pasted on. The room itself is an advertisement; and in fact the kind of advertisement which was created by spatial means. Inside the room there is an artificial tension. So much of what composes our daily spatial reality is absent. Everything that could compete with the effect of colour has been extracted from this reality. Apart from the necessary seating there is no reference to human proportions. In this room there are no shapes, no materials which would allow volume perception. There are no details. The result is the sensation of a two-dimensional room as in a hyper-realistically-reconstructed comic, or as if one had entered the synthetic world of a video clip. All that remains of everyday reality is a wafer-thin surface. The room consists of colour and light. The diminution of spatial reality is not intended to be abstract but rather elementary in order to be able to reach the essential power of the colour in spite of its diminution; the project is not an installation but continues to be committed to everyday use.

The main intention was to set the direct expression of the colourfulness against surroundings dominated by shades of grey.

Photographs: Christian Kerez

The shop is designed as a direct expression of colour in contrast to the dark and grey surroundings. The elements used daily have been reduced to a minimum expression in order to create a neutral interior to highlight the powerful use of colour.

Except for the necessary chairs, nothing suggests the functional nature of the elements of which the shop is made up or relates them to human proportions.

David Chipperfield
Joseph Menswear
London, UK

David Chipperfield's firm was commissioned to transform an old four-storey office building into the first Joseph boutique for men. In the conception of the project there was a predominant desire to transfer to an architectural language the philosophy of austerity, purity and elegance that characterises the firm. The ground floor and first floor, which occupy a total of 400 sq m, house the different collections of clothes and accessories. The second floor had previously been restored by Joseph Ettegui, the client and owner of Joseph stores, to house the show-room and the offices.

The glazed facades of double height –6 meters– act as a shop window and unify the sales space from the exterior, while a steel mesh wraps the second floor of the facades that open onto Ixworth Place and Sloane Avenue, where the access to the store is located. The external cladding of the building reflects the personality of the spaces that it encloses: the glass of the lower levels reveals the open character of the exhibition area and facilitates the dialogue between the interior of the establishment and the street, while the privacy of the show-room is reinforced behind a metal veil.

The floors that house the boutique were completely renewed. The ground floor is now an irregular space and the first floor has adopted an L-shape. The spaces are articulated along an axis, which greatly facilitates the work of the shop assistants. For the interior of the boutique, simplicity and restraint were used in the choice of materials and colours. The result is, however, very forceful. Petra Serena was used for the floor, and the vertical walls were smoothed and painted white. The fitting rooms feature careful details. The space is illuminated by lamps fitted in the ceiling and spotlights on racks. On the ground floor, lamps sunk into the floor welcome the customers. A spiral staircase of steel and wood connects the two floors of the boutique and forms an emblematic element of the space.

Photographs: Richard Bryant / ARCAID

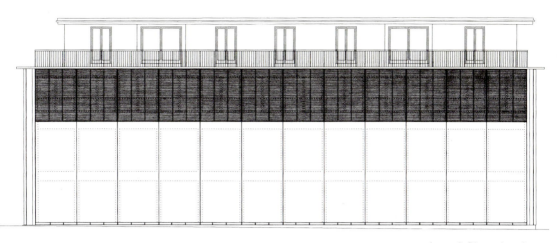

Ixworth Place elevation

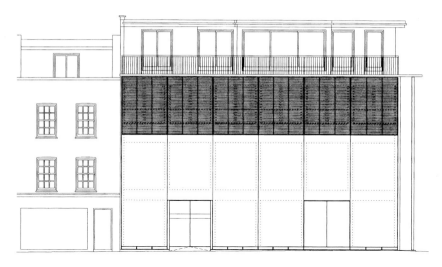

Sloane Avenue elevation

Joseph Store rises in its environment as a light metal cube that contrasts both chromatically and stylistically with the surrounding buildings.
The glazing of the ground floor and first floor exposes their structure, while a metal mesh encloses the area housing the offices and show-room.

Longitudinal section

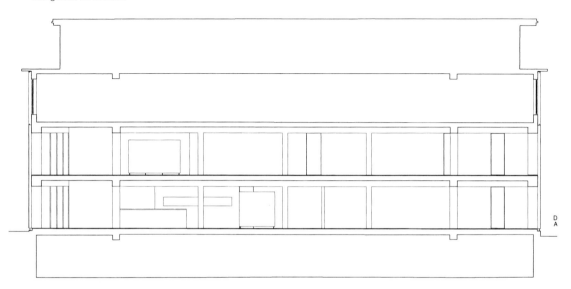

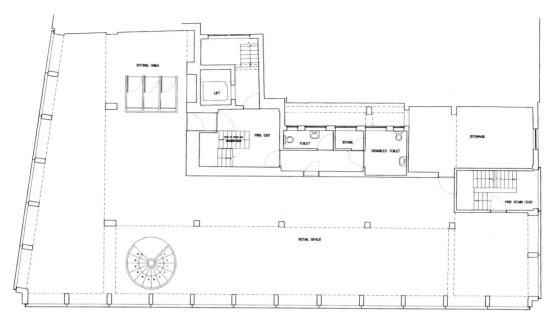

First floor plan

Ground floor plan

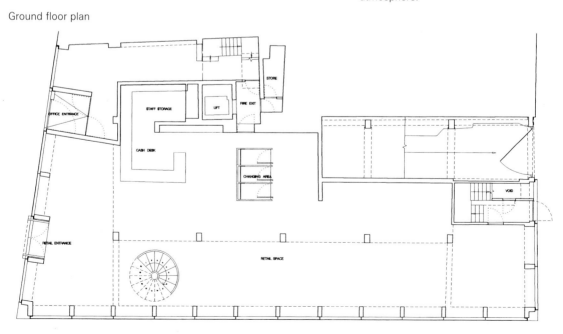

The interior of the boutique has been conceived as an austere and monumental space, dominated by the large spiral staircase that connects the two floors. The columns give rhythm and dynamism to the atmosphere.

Cross-section

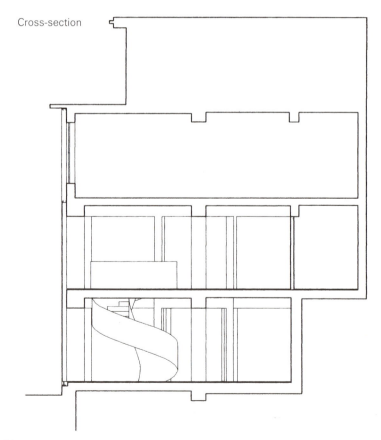

Marta de Rezio
Kickers
Milano, Italy

The new Italian office of the Kickers footwear firm has been located in Milan, in an old building devoted to industrial use. This type of space was especially suitable for housing both the public and private spaces of the firm: the offices on the first floor, and the warehouse and shop on the ground floor.

The old premises of Caprona Aerei offered a great advantage: four glazed facades that allowed a large amount of natural light to enter the building. These extraordinary lighting conditions influenced the decision to empty the space, eliminating the internal divisions and treating the interior walls as if they were translucent divisions. These were made in wood and vitreous resin, a material that acts as a catalyst and diffuser of the natural light. Through the planimetric layout of these walls, new perspectives have been obtained that act as guides to the different routes and allow the visitor to guess the depth of the spaces. The decision to transmit the image of a luminous box is stated by means of the material used in the floor: brilliant white epoxy resin forming a homogeneous surface. The introduction of notes of colour, warm orange tones, is reserved for the walls that serve as a background for the perspective of the long circulation spaces and the graphic play of the mobile wall that contains, on the opposite side, the display of the footwear.

The general lighting of the offices consists of small, industrial-type suspended lights in satin-finish aluminium, while each table is illuminated locally by desk lamps. In the circulation spaces large fitted spotlights with low-consumption bulbs were used. The show-room is lighted by suspended, industrial-type halogen lamps. The display wall is illuminated by swivelling iodine lamps that do not alter the colours of the products.

Photographs: Margherita del Piano

The rehabilitation and recovery of the building was based on historiographic analysis of the typologies of industrial architecture, incorporating and highlighting the aspects that adapted most naturally to the desired functional characteristics and image.

Floor plan

The architects have unified a space that conjugates diverse uses by using light, colour and bright, clear materials. While bright colours have been used for the walls of the circulation areas, in the show-room white is dominant and the products on display are the main features of the space.

Roger Hirsch
IS Industries Stationery Store
New York, USA

In the project for Industries Stationery Store, the architects have created a flexible and stimulating space, a window that captures the attention of the pedestrians and attracts them to the interior of the store without detracting from the product on display, and all this with a budget of US$ 25,000 and in only three months from the conception of the design to the completion of the work. The interior structure was stripped of all the added elements and only the old brick walls and the irregular wooden floor were respected. The main display elements are in natural maple wood, unpolished aluminium and untreated wooden boards. The distribution of these elements emphasises the long, narrow shape of the space and enhances the product on display.

A maple wood counter of almost 5.5 metres, in the form of a long box supported on aluminium legs with a square section, seems to float on the floor. Inside it conceals all the facilities of the store, such as the computer (of which only the monitor is visible), the cash register and the space for storing bags and gift wrapping. This counter also acts as a display, and its exaggerated length induces the client to travel along the long, narrow space.

The system of steel shelves running along the brick wall is suspended from the ceiling and rests on the floor, leaving two display surfaces, one at counter level and another at eye level. Papers and envelopes hang from a steel band that runs along the rear of the shelf. The papers and envelopes on display are attached to the shelf by small magnets, and can thus be easily renewed. This display system is illuminated by a strip of halogen lamps inserted in the front rail of the upper shelf. The electric cables of the shelves and the counter are hidden inside tubular aluminium structures. The front display area that acts as a shop window houses a sculptural system composed of a stack of wooden boards crossed by two steel bars that go from floor to ceiling. At the opposite end of the store a cloth screen of 2.74x3.04 m conceals 2.4 m fluorescent tubes, creating the effect of a box of light and giving clarity and brightness to the area furthest from the street.

Photographs: Patrik Rytikangas

Floor plan

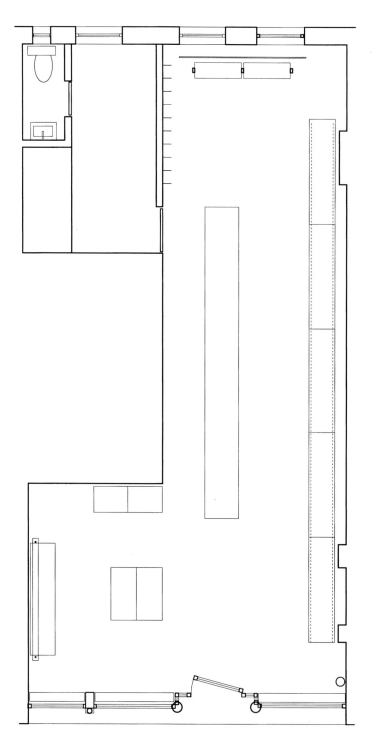

The colourful and lively shop window creates a strong impact in the environment. The products on display act as decorative elements, attracting the attention of the passers-by.

The highly geometric display elements and counter reinforce the linear nature of the space and invite the client to move along the circulation space.

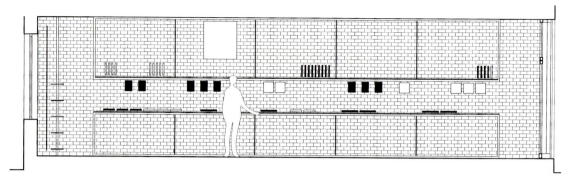

Interior elevations

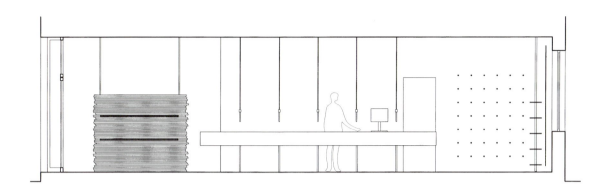

Claudio Silvestrin
Giorgio Armani Store
Paris, France

The new boutique of Giorgio Armani in Paris occupies two floors of a stately building in Place Vendôme. In this scheme, Claudio Silvestrin conceived a space that transcends minimalism and captures that eternal elegance that constitutes the essence of Place Vendôme. The correspondence between the classical elegance of the fashion designer and the sober inclinations of the architect are reflected in this space, in which the interplay of light and shade and the materials used are basic elements of the scheme.

The boutique makes contact with the street gradually. The original entrance to the building is prolonged beyond a glass door mounted on a metal frame of the same material as that used for the handles. Behind this door, a limestone wall blocks the vision of the interior of the space. One then enters a second space of transition defined by a sculptural vase of the same stone as the walls and floor. This creates the effect of continuity and sobriety that so characterise the work of Armani.

The boutique is developed on two floors. The walls and the floor, in untreated limestone, and the furniture, in Macassar mahogany, follow the same chromatic line. The furniture is defined by sumptuous materials and a careful location in the space. The mirrors are arranged in transition zones, which creates a sensation of space, whereas the sculptural mahogany chairs reinforce the idea of the geometric interplay. The lighting, consisting of lights fitted into the ceiling and walls, becomes another construction element that defines the different spaces and highlights the garments on display.

The materials used play a very important role in this scheme. Austere elements corresponding to the simplicity and elegance of Armani's designs were used. The elementary architecture of light and shade and the purity of the forms seem to be chiselled into the stone. One could say that time stood still at the precise moment when Place Vendôme was created.

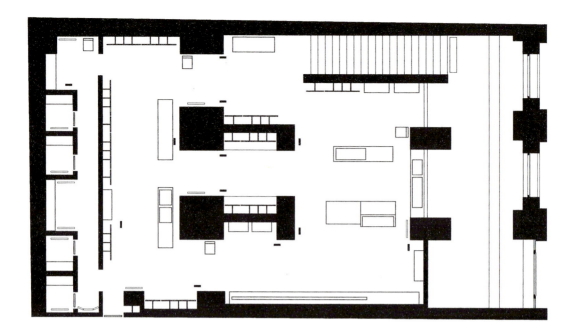

First floor plan

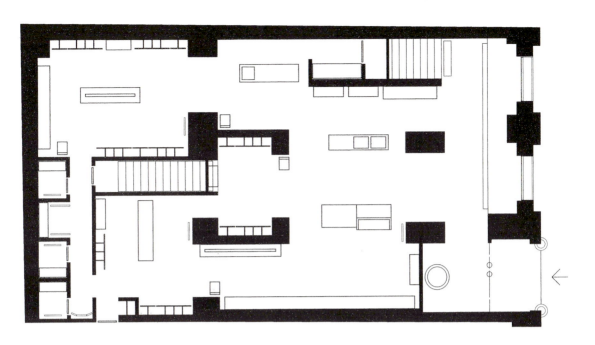

Ground floor plan

The boutique is defined by two basic elements: the materials and the lighting. The first are limited to limestone for the floor and walls and Macassar mahogany for the display elements.

The fitted lamps in the ceiling and walls create a chiaroscuro effect, modelling the stone and falling on the garments on display, the main characters of this theatrical stage.

Eric Raffy
Cabin Racing Team
Tokyo, Japan

The Japanese tobacco company decided to use the French talent and sensitivity of Eric Raffy in order to design the firm's showroom in Tokyo. It is a space for promoting the Cabin brand of cigarettes, the sponsor of the Cabin Racing Team Formula 3000 and motorcycling team. The aim of the facility was to reflect the identity of the brand architectonically, based on a dynamic but relaxed idea of competition. In addition to this image, Eric Raffy played with concepts such as light, movement and fluidity, which allowed him to conceive this facility and to create a stimulating and relaxed atmosphere.

The showroom is located on the ground floor of a three-storey building belonging to the Japanese tobacco company. The facility is organised around three spaces with essential functions: a space for sales of accessories and products associated with the brand: a communications space that fulfils the dual function of receiving visitors and providing permanent information on the activities of the brand; and a display space with the colours of the Cabin Racing Team for the promotion of Formula 3000 and motorcycling. There are three essential themes in the brand image: The kinetic images of cigarette smoke, the car races and the calm concept of the void, which is deeply rooted in Japanese culture and tradition.

A large, undulating wall unifies the space and gives it fluidity. It was conceived as a white silk veil moving in harmonious waves. This wall envelops the whole showroom and highlights the objects on display. Two large fans reinforce the idea of gentle movement. The furniture was specially designed by Eric Raffy for the showroom. Its forms match the "veil", with gentle, flexible and dynamic curves. The reception and sales counters, and the plinth for presenting the racing motorbike, are made in sycamore wood with a light-coloured grain. On the light-coloured wood floor, red fitted lamps guide the visitor through this universe, where harmony and dynamism engage in a seductive dialogue.

Photographs: Hikaru Suzuki

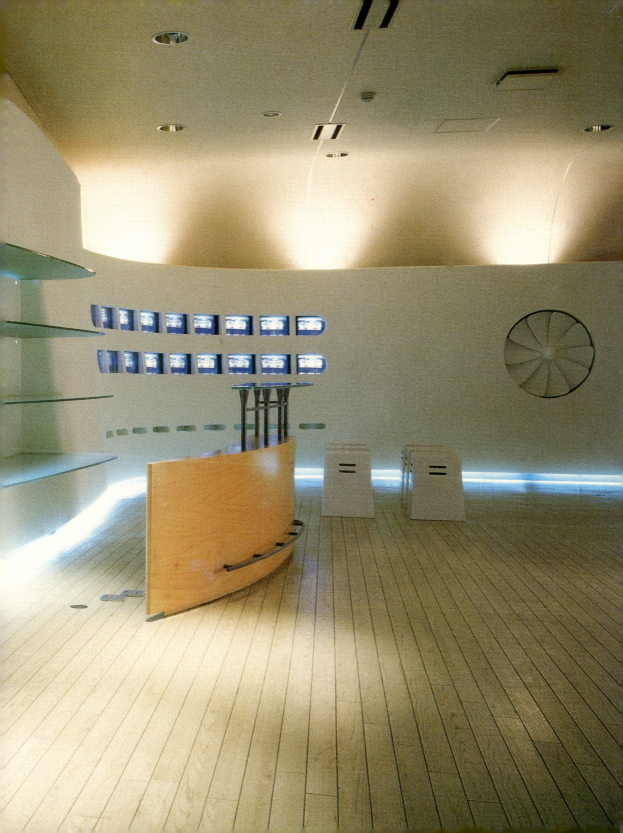

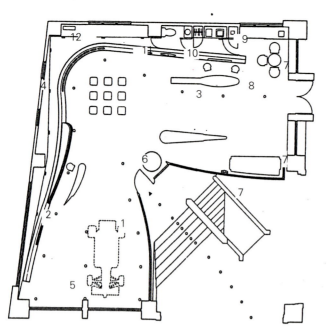

1. Access
2. Reception-information area
3. Counter
4. Video-communication
5. Formula 3000 exhibition
6. Racing motorbike exhibition
7. Garment exhibition
8. Business reception area
9. Sales
10. Kitchenette-dressing rooms
11. Toilets
12. Storage

Blue glass shelves convert the "veil" of fibrous plasterwork into a display element. Also fitted in this wall are two large fans and a mosaic of television monitors that show non-stop images of motor competitions.

The carefully studied use of light gives the space a dreamlike quality. The fitted lamps in the floor, the spotlights hidden behind the wall and the tubes provide indirect lighting that immerses the visitor in a timeless space.

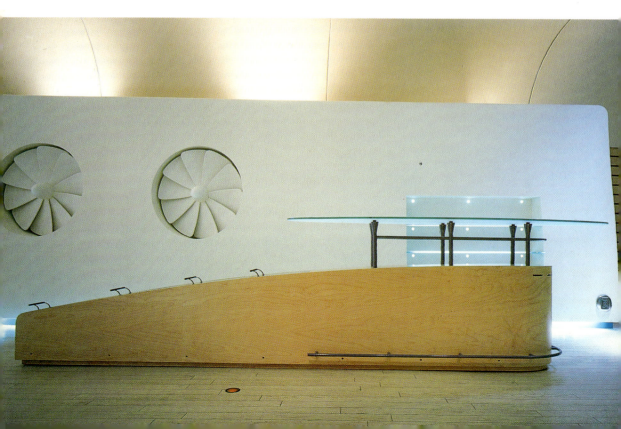

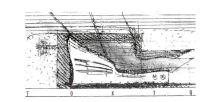
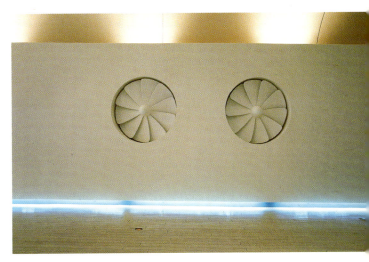
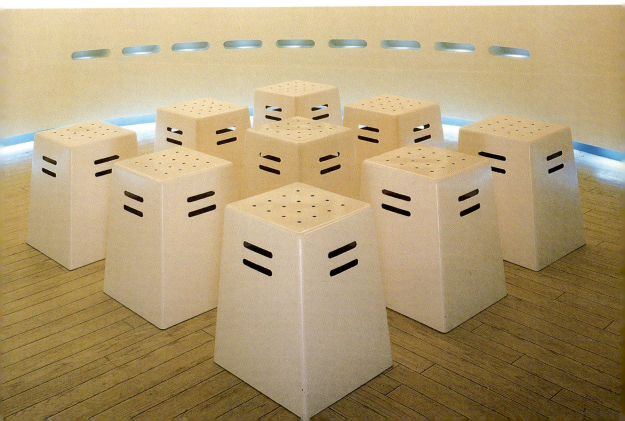

Claudio Silvestrin
Starkmann's Office / Johan Menswear Shop
Boston, USA / Graz, Austria

Johan Menswear Shop is in the heart of Graz's traditional shopping quarter. Its interior consists of two long narrow spaces with vaulted ceiling. These two spaces were originally rather pokey and gloomy but have been transformed into a streamlined, futuristic interior. Yet, although it is as modern as the interior of a space shuttle, it appears as though Silvestrin has excavated the site, added light and revealed a timeless cave, its serenity perfectly preserved and its monoliths intact.

Ceiling, walls, shelving, display tables and units are rendered in grey greenish pigmented plaster; the floor is covered with concrete. The two sections of the shop consist of the main display area on one side, where the space's perspective is emphasised by the 15 m long stepped wooden display counter which stretches from wall to wall in front of a screen of back-lit satin glass and offers a place to sit. The other section is visually separate and contains the same pigmented plaster. These three playful structures shield the body but end at neck-level at the top. They are illuminated by natural light entering through a horizontal cut carved in the ceiling to the floor above.

Starkmann's Office is a 6,000 sq ft interior transformation of a 1960's warehouse situated in the Massachusetts countryside, half an hour by car from Boston. Despite a modest budget, the office is a rare example of how minimalist architecture can also function in working environments.

The architect's arrangement of theatrical screens, dwarf walls, stretched openings and elementary material accommodates the necessary functions and technology. Yet the presence of technology is not overpowering to the eye; indeed it is virtually invisible. Space, light, materials, computers, books, art, nature and people are perceived as a nonfragmented order.

Photographs: Tessa Robins

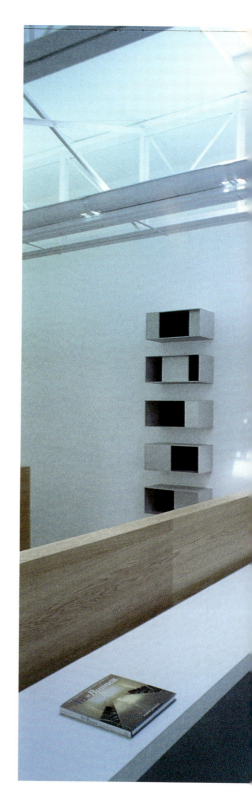

Starkmann's Office

The whole paraphernalia of an office is visible. Through austere finishes a total balance between visual purity and functional efficiency has been achieved.

Johan Menswear Shop

The lighting comes mainly from halogen lamps placed along the whole perimeter of the shop and supplementary ones hidden behind a satin-finish glass panel embedded in the wall.
The narrowest part of the shop has been intentionally cramped even more by the curve of the roof.

Lazzarini Pickering Architetti
Fendi Boutique
Roma, Italy

The new store in Rome is the exponent of the aesthetic renewal of the Fendi boutiques. The new international image of the firm is dark, architectonic, luxurious. It was born as a reaction to the growing uniformity of the white and monotonous international boutiques that are all practically the same. The objective of the project consisted in creating an architectural system that was beyond the mere sum of hangers and shelves that is so common in many establishments. A spatial whole rather than a series of adjoining atmospheres. All the display units (shelves, hanger systems, tables, etc.) are conceived as architectural elements that are in proportion with the space… long, sculptural and silent bodies, with shelves over ten metres long.

The store is dominated by dark colours: the floor is made of steel, while the walls are brown or black. It is a sober store, an invisible space in which all the elements interact three-dimensionally. The system of panels that clad the walls conceal all the facilities (air conditioning, electric connections, sockets). Between the panels are guides on which the display elements are supported, leaving the panels totally free.

The idea of the shop window has disappeared. The store is exhibited as a whole, with all the garments visible through the windows. From the exterior one sees a group of customers and clothes that move inside the store. Those who are inside observe the exterior as if it were an exhibition.

Photographs: Matteo Piazza

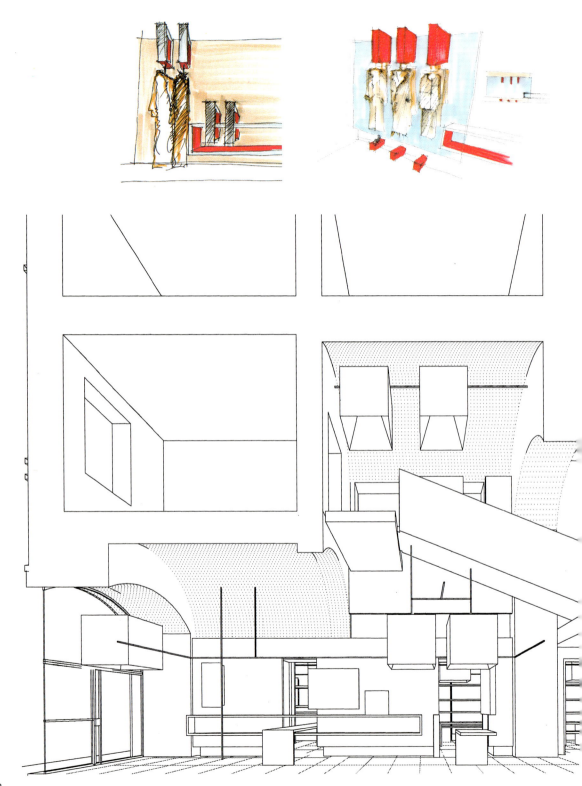

Although the materials are austere, the dark panels and the untreated steel of blue-black tones create a luxurious background that highlights the quality of the garments.

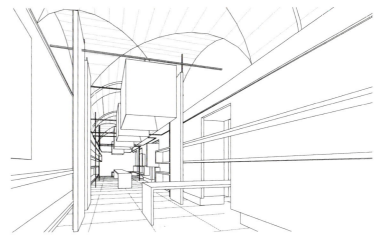

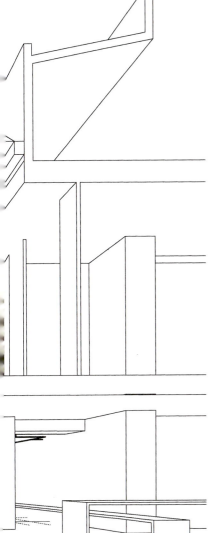

The interior of the boutique is conceived as a sculptural space, with a constant intersection of planes that multiplies the surfaces and allows the customers to perceive the articles in a dynamic and random display. The arrangement of garments is informal and sculptural, filling the store with an apparent disorder that encourages the customers to touch the clothes and to try them on.

Ground floor plan

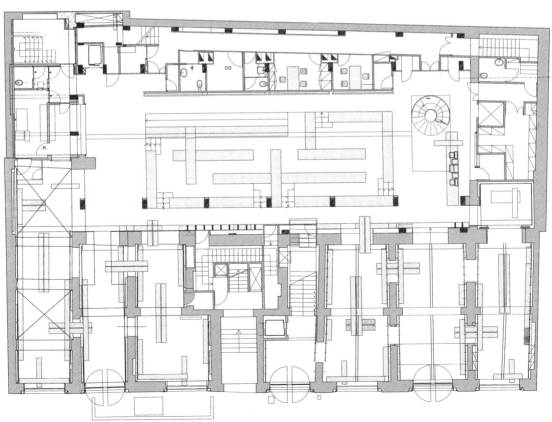

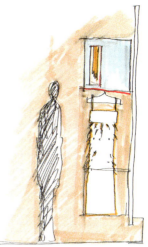

The lighting of the boutique is solved by means of directional spotlights in the ceiling. The result is a deliberately theatrical atmosphere in which the display elements are integrated with the architectural elements, forming an intricate combination of volumes.

I. Vilela, J. Armas & R. Ruano
Farmacia Tenoya
Las Palmas de Gran Canaria, Islas Canarias. Spain

The designers of this popular drugstore in Grand Canary wished to imbue it with the type of unique ambience which is not usually found in establishments of its kind. A rare freshness —very welcome in this hot clime— greets visitors, whose attention is immediately drawn to a centrally-placed fountain which visually dominates the main space.

The 9-meter-long, half-moon shaped service counter is divided into three tiered surface planes where customers can comfortably place their bags and other belongings. The front face of the service counter bears the drugstore's insignia. Full use was made of the space below the counter by installing medicine drawers and two refrigerators, one placed at each end, for medications that must be kept cold.

The walls are of 70-cm-thick reinforced concrete, to which is added a 9 cm skin on both faces. The material used for this skin comes directly from Brazil: rich mineral stones of quartz, mica and feldspar, which acquire particular brilliance when light is shone on them.

The smallest stones have been used to fill in the spaces between the larger ones, giving individuality and personality to the natural color of the stone.

The columns are sufficiently pronounced so as to separate the various departments: pharmaceuticals, cosmetics, animal care and hygiene, for example. The capitals of the columns are adorned with the symbols of Upper and Lower Egypt, the papyrus plant and lotus flower, which are in turn fitted with concealed, upward-facing torchiers for indirect lighting.

The project's emblematic piece is the oval-shaped fountain, of some four meters in length and more than 2.3 meters in width, which provides distinct perspectives on all sides. It is the anchoring component of the entire surface, creating, along with the sound of the water, a fresh and idyllic atmosphere.

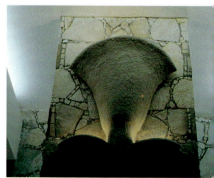

Photographs: Jerónimo Armas

Main elevation

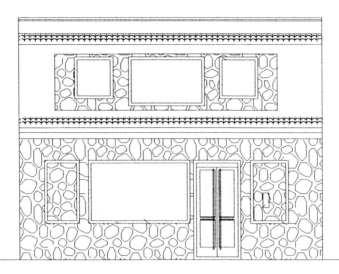

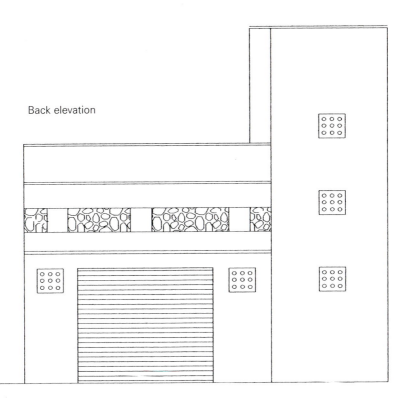

Back elevation

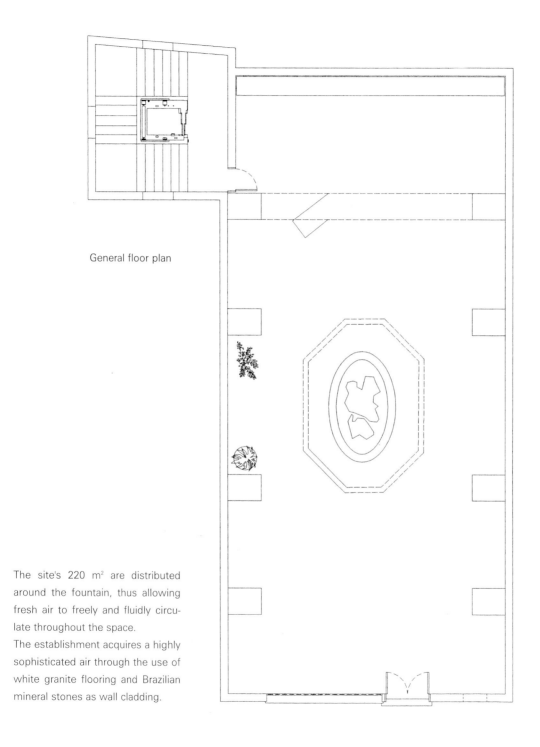

General floor plan

The site's 220 m² are distributed around the fountain, thus allowing fresh air to freely and fluidly circulate throughout the space.
The establishment acquires a highly sophisticated air through the use of white granite flooring and Brazilian mineral stones as wall cladding.

Michael Gabellini
Boutique Jil Sander
Milano, Italy

This is not the first time that Michael Gabellini has worked for Jil Sander. His team had previously been hired for the design of another boutique in San Francisco and of some offices and a showroom in Hamburg for this same company. This project called for a single-story design for a shop in which to display the women's and men's clothing and accessory collections. The design concept gave precedence to simplicity and comfort for the client, who can view and try on the collections on display. The boutique's only street entrance is located on the facade between four wide display windows which entice the passerby to enter the locale and view its wares, while at the same time providing the space with an abundance of natural light, the presence of which reinforces the compression of certain areas and suggests a continuity between the boutique's interior and its surroundings.

All interior vertical faces have been polished and painted white, conferring a bright, luminous effect on the space. Built-in lamps placed directly above each display highlight the quality of the clothes and guide the customer through the boutique. A steel staircase connects the showroom floor to a small storage room in the basement where the merchandise not on display is kept.

The display fixtures are an integral part of the interior architecture of this project. The simple and elegant pieces - some steel, others in wood - are distributed throughout the space in such a way as to remain unnoticed, thereby granting the clothing and accessories all their deserved central importance. Thus, the merchandise is never eclipsed by its surrounding context. Rather, its quality is enhanced and the client feels comfortable to enjoy the shopping experience.

Photographs: Alberto Piovano

For this project, the architect designed a space with pure, bare surfaces where the display units, in metal and wood, are sculptural bodies, elements where the clothes are exhibited.

Patrick Genard
Sephora
Barcelona, Spain

This scheme involved the remodelling for commercial use of the interior of the premises located in Avinguda de la Llum, in "El Triangle" shopping centre of Barcelona. The premises are located in a double space. One part is in a space known as Avinguda de la Llum (the basement), and the other occupies part of the building of "El Triangle" shopping centre (the ground floor and mezzanine). The premises are on three levels with double access on the ground floor: direct access from the exterior on Carrer Pelai, and access from the common areas of the shopping centre. The ground floor is used as an access to the premises through a double height hall that communicates with the basement by means of a double escalator and a lift for the disabled. The basement, which occupies the whole length of Avinguda de la Llum, will be devoted to commercial use. At the sides of this space are the complementary areas such as: wardrobes, toilets for employees and the public, services and staff rooms.

Sephora is indicated from the entrance by a colonnade that is reflected to infinity, leading toward the vault of mirrors, a magnificent showcase that constitutes its architectural identity. A red carpet is an element of orientation and decoration, distributing the main corridors of the store. The floor of black and white marble and the black furniture confirm the sober and luxurious expression of the interior architecture.

From the street to the product, everything has been conceived to give the customers autonomy and rapid orientation, so that they can linger at will or seek guidance. The store is spatially distributed according to three different universes, three beauty trades: perfumery, make-up and beauty care.

The scheme takes the aesthetic concept of Sephora to an extreme: materials, furniture, design and scenery reflect the black and white chromatics of the other stores of the chain, whilst highlighting the architectural identity of Avinguda de la Llum.

Photographs: Jordi Miralles

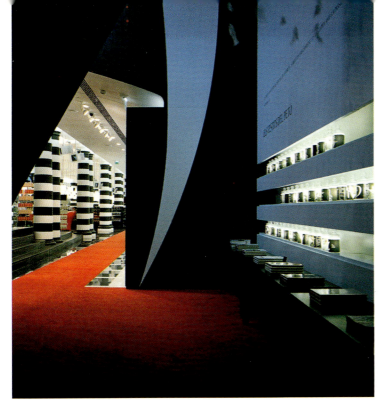

One enters the store through a row of black and white grooved columns, reflected to infinity by mirror panels dotted with elliptical windows that allow one to see perfumes and monitors. The sides of the corridor and of the ceiling are also lined with mirrors that reflect the colonnade to infinity, upwards and downwards.

The old double colonnade has been restored and painted in the characteristic black and white motif of Sephora. A circulation circuit of red carpet runs along the sides of the store.

The general lighting of the store is provided by 16 rows of suspended lights per vault and lines of fluorescent tubes that directly illuminate the curved drop ceiling of the side galleries. In this area the perfumes are displayed on shelving units of black painted veneer and glass with integrated lighting.

Studio Baciocchi
Miu Miu
Milano, Italy

The impact of the Miú Miu boutique in its environment, the Corso Venezia of Milán, immediately defines the rigorous linear philosophy of the architectural project: the shop window opens up in a facade clad with grey cement slabs, framing the geometries and forms of an interior space of 400 sqm developed horizontally.

Roberto Bacciochi has created large volumes divided by panels that define the diverse display areas and always leave spaces open at the intersection points with the walls and ceiling. The different levels of the store are easily accessed by steps and a ramp. The result is a space of great unity, free of superfluous decorative elements.

The choice of materials reflects a desire for contrast rather than homogeneity or balance. Grey cement has been used in the floor and the counter, while polished aluminium is reserved for the display units –shelves, cabinets and hangers– and for the benches, which are consoles covered by leather cushions and attached to the canvas-lined walls. The walls and ceiling are plastered in white, while the colour red defines the panels that divide the space and serve as a frame for the garments on display. The interior of the display units is also painted red. This colour is only used on certain surfaces, marking elements of special relevance and contributing dynamism to the space. The display models hang from the ceiling, illuminated at the lower part of the bust. The white plastered fitting rooms have etched glass doors. Lights fitted into longitudinal slashes in the ceiling illuminate the space and enhance the quality of the garments. The result is a unique and stimulating atmosphere, the perfect support for the MIU MIU line.

Photographs: Alberto Piovano

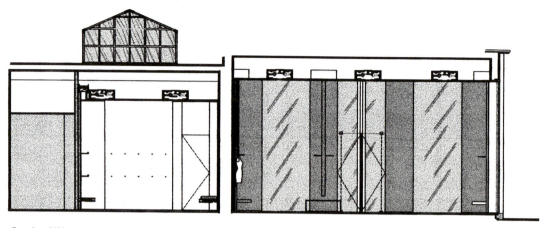

Section NN

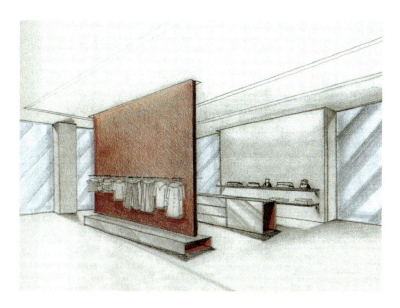

Colour plays a major role in this project. The red and grey form a vibrant palette that serves as a backdrop to the garments on display and defines the route through the different spaces of the boutique.

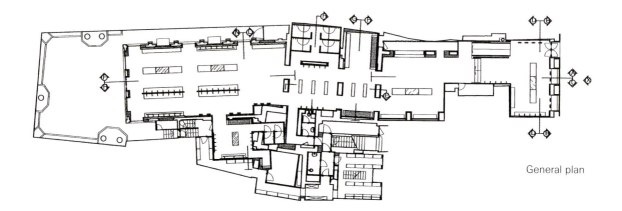

General plan

Steps and a ramp have been used to connect the different levels of the long, deep floor and give the space dynamism.

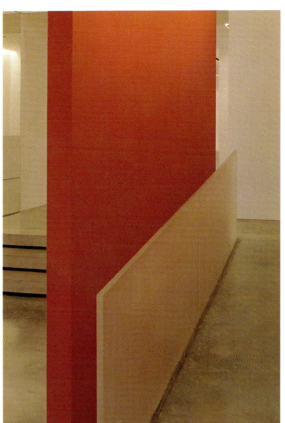

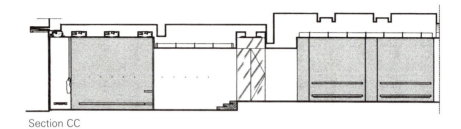

Section CC

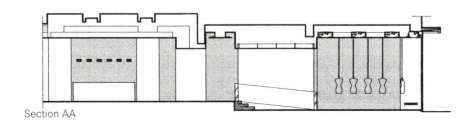

Section AA

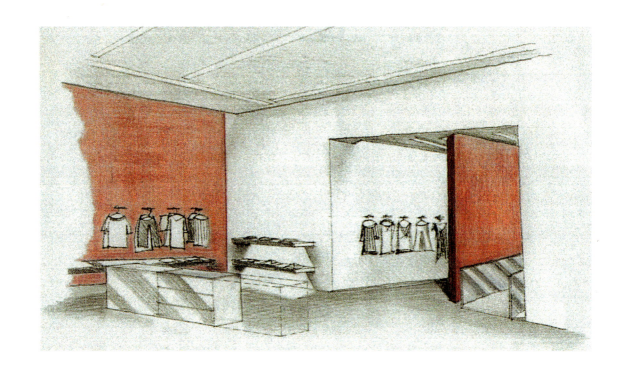

Pepa Poch
Peluquerías Salva G
Barcelona, Spain

The clients' brief called for the reform and construction of two hairdressing salons in buildings which had been designated as historically significant set in the city's old quarter. The idea was to create open spaces above the entrance, preserving the wood beams and sturdy iron columns.

The first site, of approximately 220 m^2, is on a street of very little traffic in the *Barrio Gótico*, where a number of new designers' shops and trendy bars have sprouted up. This shop has kept the original distribution, with a double-height main space, which is free of vertical divisions, the entirety of which is visible from the entryway. Here, there is a waiting area next to a large picture window and the reception counter with lighted panels. Stairs lead to the mezzanine, where the sinks, tanning beds and hairstyling stations are located. From the entry, the visitor descends to the lower level, where there are also hairdressing stations, as well as a lab, storage area and office.

This shop makes its mark not so much for its spatial distribution as for an eye-catching blend of decorative styles.

The second shop, of 60 m^2, follows the same criteria. It is located in the recently revived neighborhood called the Born, an area known for its nightlife, restaurants and shops and for being a pleasing area for a leisurely stroll. It is a narrow, yet open, volume of considerable height, with a loft, where carriages were probably originally kept. The original door and iron inner door welcome visitors to the premises. From here, one can easily see the area for washing and styling hair and a shelf unit, which serves as a divider between sections. There are also toilets and a storage area.

The rounded steel stations and unusual mirrors with their frames incrusted with tiny light bulbs capture the attention.

Seen from the street, the "chill-out" loft has been set aside as a relaxing waiting area. The walls are lined in wood panels, pieced together as if in a puzzle.

Poch and Mirallvell have opted for an eclectic decorating style in both shops, where the style of the 50s, 60s and 70s and post-modern design are intermingled: reupholstered second-hand furniture, mosaic floors, ostentatious lamps and custom-made illuminated furniture and mirrors.

The original wood facade has been left intact. The picture window provides a quick glimpse of the interior.

The top photograph shows the huge piece with lighted panels where products are on display in the reception area. The structure of this display case is iron.

Front door of the second branch of the shop, opened in 2001. Two iron inner doors, which serve as a contrast as well as security, were added to the original wood facade.

The walls are painted with a 50s-inspired motif. This gentle background is a contrast to the mirrors with their tiny light bulbs embedded into the frames.

The "chill-out" loft, a perfect spot for relaxing, has wooden beams and an iron column. The walls are clad in wood, serving at the same time as a puzzle.

From this height, one can enjoy a panoramic view of the establishment.

Claudio Nardi
Ferre' Jeans Boutique
Roma, Italy

In Piazza di Spagna of Roma, Ferre' Jeans is located in a space strongly characterized by volumes typical of the old commercial locales of the Capitoline historic center.

The store window, situated on the long side of the Piazza, offers the observer a small screen, beyond which the views of the surfaces within lure the passerby in for a closer look. Here, the eye wanders along the outfitted walls, the staircase, the visual background and the focal point of the setting.

The double volume of its containing space is paneled entirely in an immense graphic and connects the two levels of similar architectonic characteristics, although diverse in their sales functions (accessories on the ground floor and men's and women's wear on the first).

Each individual element of the tectonic constituents (giant-size photography, wall-panels, display tables) strives to be a protagonist. At the same time, the visual perspective takes center stage, functioning in conjunction with the design of the ceiling at the back, the spotlighting, the texturing of the large wall panels and the cement effect of the flooring.

The result obtained is a sales floor where the strength of the Ferre' Jean image is thoroughly manifested, while still valuing the existing architectonic scheme and conserving the distinct historical memory of the site.

Photographs: Studio Nardi

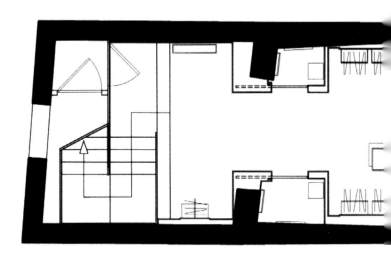
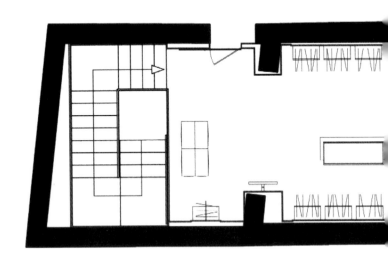

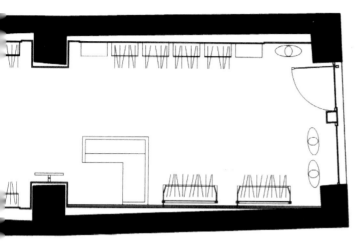

Ground floor plan

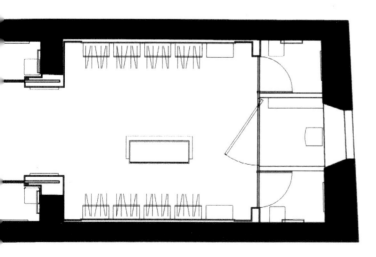

First floor plan

The store window offers the observer a small screen, beyond which the views of the surfaces within lure the passerby in for a closer look. Here, the eye wanders along the outfitted walls, the staircase, the visual background and the focal point of the setting.

Ramon Esteve
Farrutx Palma
Palma de Mallorca, Spain

The present project is a shop for a brand of shoes in the city of Palma, Mallorca. The premises not only had to house a store but also to act as the flagship of the company, representing its values. The brief was to restore commercial premises located in a building with historical value in the Passeig des Born, a shopping area of Palma. The ground plan was originally rectangular, a free container of flat walls and right angles that the architect respected, treating the walls with affection and giving back to them the dignity of their nakedness.

The facade was restored, and the destroyed part was reconstructed from moulds taken from the symmetrical side of the facade, using the same type of stone as the original and the same manual procedure.

The access from the street coincides with the only opening in the facade, becoming at the same time the entrance and the window. The whole area of the shop is thus transformed into an immense display for the products which can be seen from the pavement through a 2 cm thick glass door weighing almost 250 kg. Worked by a movement sensor, a mechanism triggers the silent motor to slide the heavy glass sheet, which is absorbed by the threshold as though it were a thin membrane. At the back, three panes of translucent glass are illuminated from the rear. Fitted without frames, clean from top to bottom, housed simply in the stone of the floor and the plaster of the ceiling, they give the sensation that the space extends beyond the limits of the premises.

The furniture forms an integral part of the architecture of the shop, consisting of free-standing elements, solid 12 cm thick slabs of polished Bateig stone that rest on a cross of the same material. The location of the benches divides the store into sub-spaces, aligning everything for pure contemplation. Organising in a space the habitual elements of a shop, creating an atmosphere that invites one to tranquillity and conjugating the building tradition with the latest technological innovations is an exercise of synthesis. Clearing a wall of mouldings and skirtings is a declaration of principles. Controlling the light by illuminating each corner without leaving a bulb or spotlight visible is a contained homage to the architecture, removing from the forefront anything that is not essential.

The access door to the store, a sliding 20 mm sheet of laminated safety glass absorbed into the wall without frames, acts as a shop window, blurring the limits between the interior and the exterior of the space.

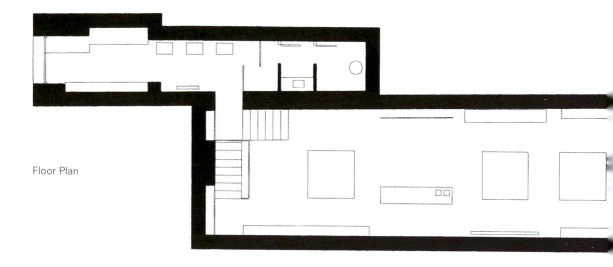

Floor Plan

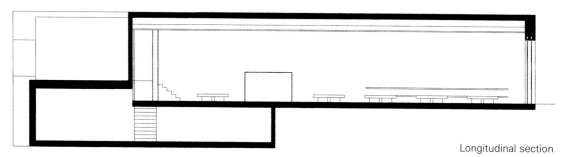

Longitudinal section

The layout of the display elements marks the different sub-spaces of the store. Austerity and chromatic restraint were dominant in the choice of materials: benches and paving of Bateig sandstone, Wengué wood furniture and suspended shelves and accessory elements of stainless steel with a burnished finish.

Peter Marino Assoc. Architects
Giorgio Armani
New York, USA

The proposed alteration was to erect a new structural steel frame utilising the existing foundations. The building height was dictated to align with the existing brownstones to the north. The new four-story building was clad in cream-coloured French limestone with very large expanses of stone and glass. The 10'x10' glass panels were intended to allow light diffusion by means of theatrical scrims in the high-ceilinged rooms. Inside, French limestone walls and ebonized limestone stairs enclose the ornamental stair, rising from the first to the fourth floor.

Individual sales room walls were distinguished by French limestone and bleached cerused curly hickory or bleached anigre, except for the fourth floor, where they are a combination of bleached anigre and French limestone. Floors are either ebonized French limestone wood with custom-made silver gray or espresso brown woven linen carpets. New heating, ventilation and air conditioning, sprinklers, plumbing, electrical systems and new elevators have been installed.

Photographs: Peter Aaron /Esto

In the interior both the floor and the internal partitions have been fully clad with cream-coloured French limestone.

The wall supporting the interior staircase communicating the four floors of the premises reveals the outline of the staircase that it conceals.

The building combines a small range colours and materials: the cream colour of the limestone, the dark wood, and the dark grey and dark brown of the made-to-measure carpets.

Claudio Nardi
Dolce & Gabbana / D&G
New York City, USA

Claudio Nardi headed the projects for the two boutiques which Dolce & Gabbana have opened in New York. This was no unjustified choice: his firm had been commissioned to design the private residence of the two Italian designers.

In spite of their differences, the Manhattan and Soho boutiques share the same conceptual design, that of adaptation to the surroundings while nonetheless maintaining a very pronounced identity.

Dolce & Gabbana, the Italian company's more exclusive line, is located on Madison Avenue. A sober space was sought for this boutique, where the colours and volumes play an essential role. A clearer, more contemporary interpretation of the traditional Mediterranean culture, with its art and light, was achieved. The latter, Mediterranean light, infuses the space, penetrating the interior patio to make its way along the stone stairway which, visible from the shop window, connects the basement, lower floor (ladies' collections), first floor (men's collections), the VIP lounge and the space dedicated to the brides' collection. Special attention was given to the lighting, which displays a blend of efficiency and discretion with a general feeling of chiaroscuro. The more accessible collections, D&G, are located on West Broadway in Soho, an area which brings together a high number of young designers and secondary name brands. Since this is a highly dynamic area, it seemed appropriate to turn the boutique into yet another exterior element and move it onto the street. The shop window forms the nexus, like a large, transparent and nearly imperceptible screen which occupies the entire entrance and captures the maximum of outside light. Interior lighting combines the use of fluorescent lights and partially hidden spotlighting along the walls and ceiling. The boutique's architectural elements, of a distinct character, create a rich, white and luminous space, where the garments are the true central players.

Photographs: Studio Nardi D & G Press Office

Madison Ave.

Ground floor plan

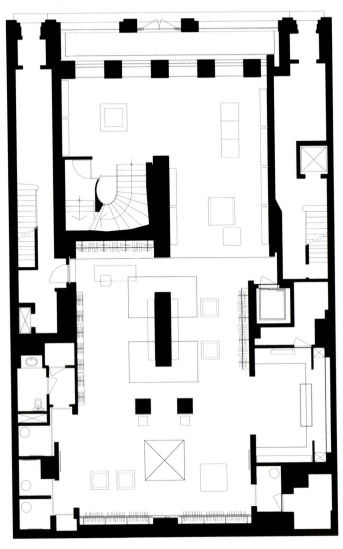

First floor plan

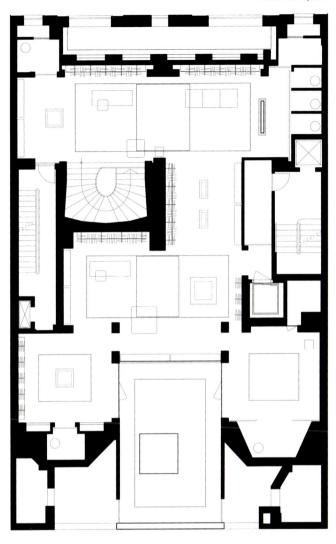

The central area of the shop features custom-designed fixtures and display cases, which are characterised by sparse cubic elements made of wood. In this space, small halogen lights reflect off the mirrors lining the walls to provide a vibrant chiaroscuro effect.

Broadway

The shop occupies two levels communicated by a staircase, with the women's clothes on the ground floor and the men's clothes on the first floor. Nardi took special care to create a space of delicate textures, in which the materials play an outstanding role: red velvet and white satin in the changing rooms, mahogany furniture and curving stainless steel on the doors and railings.

Ground floor plan

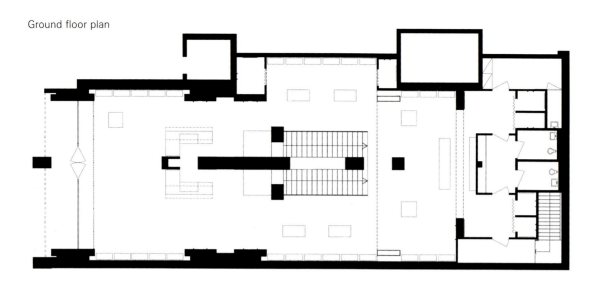

Basement floor plan

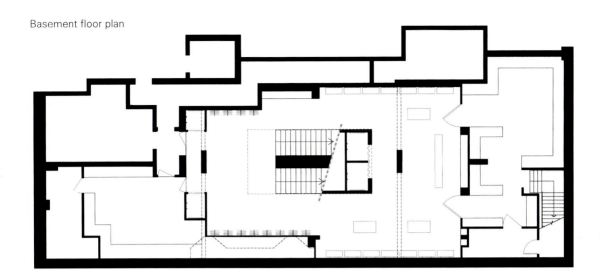

Studio Cerri & Associati
Boutique Salvini
Milano, Italy

The Salvini jeweller's shop occupies 100 sq m of the ground floor of a building on Via Montenapoleone in Milan. It is an installation of great simplicity based on the precision of the construction details and spatial transparency. The project emerged from an essential idea: that the elements should focus the visitor's attention and give character to the space. All the interventions are aimed at enhancing the jewelry, so it was decided to limit the variety of materials and colours.

The store opens up to the exterior through a stone facade interrupted by two shop windows that allow the jewels to be seen from the street. The access door is also made of glass. The customer service area is clearly longitudinal, a long circulation space in which, on both sides, the fundamental elements of the establishment have been placed: the displays and tables for serving the customers. In this area the stone of the walls has been worked, and the skirting is polished. Each of the three spaces for individualised customer attention has a small auxiliary element, a folding tray fitted into the wall with a veneer of cherry wood, a material that is also used in the tables and chairs. The opposite wall houses small cubes of steel and glass illuminated from inside by optical fibre, which are used as display units. Thanks to the austerity of materials and colours in the space, these display units become focal points.

The space is illuminated from the ceiling by fitted and hanging lights with a blue glass shade, one of the few touches of colour in the space. The design of the jeweller's shop responds to the client's wish that the space should reflect the contemporary design of the jewelry.

Photographs: Studio Amendolagine Barracchia

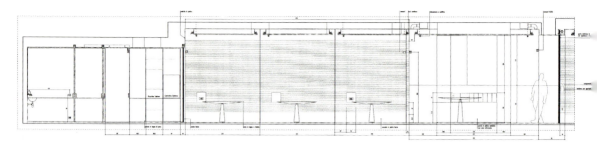

Longitudinal section AA

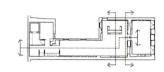

The boutique is divided into three well differentiated milieus: an area alongside the entrance (reserved for exhibiting sculptures), the shop and the private space at the back. The shop itself is subdivided into two spaces: the reception and the area for serving customers, both of which have Istria d'Orsera stone on the floor and walls, polished brass in the fitted drawer modules and white stucco on the drop ceiling.

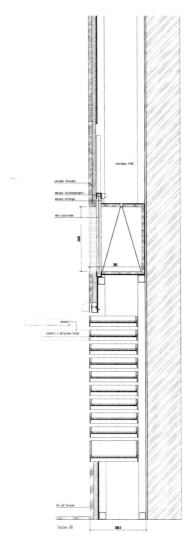

Section of the auxiliary element

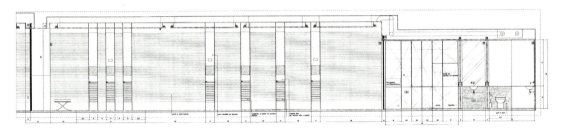

Longitudinal Section BB

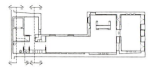

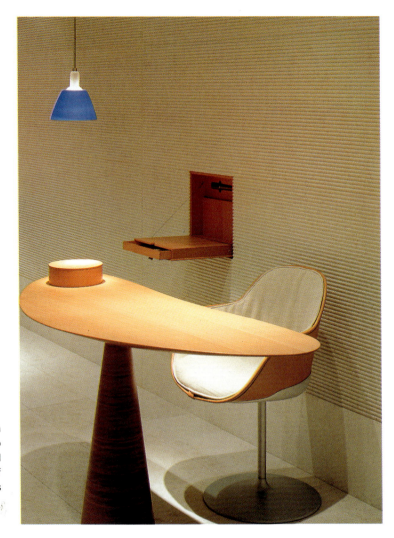

The wooden furniture constitutes a warm chromatic counterpoint to the austerity of the materials used in the project. The arrangement of the tables for serving customers emphasises the depth of the space.

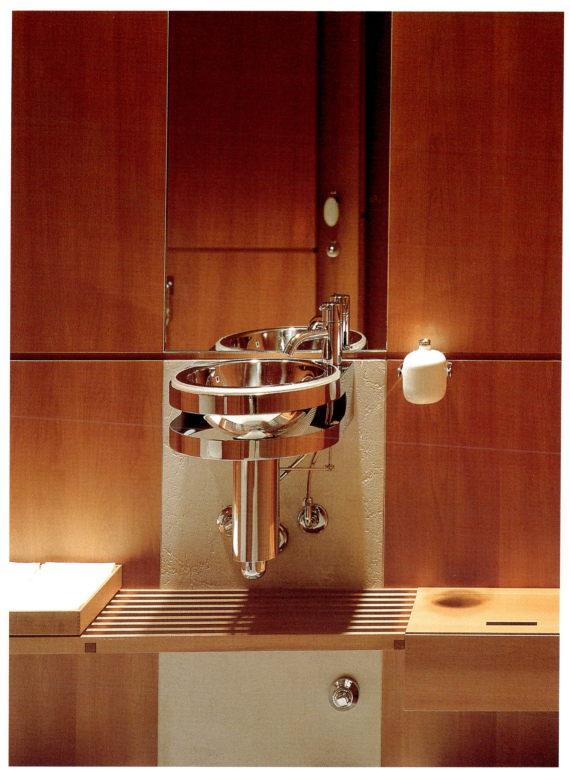

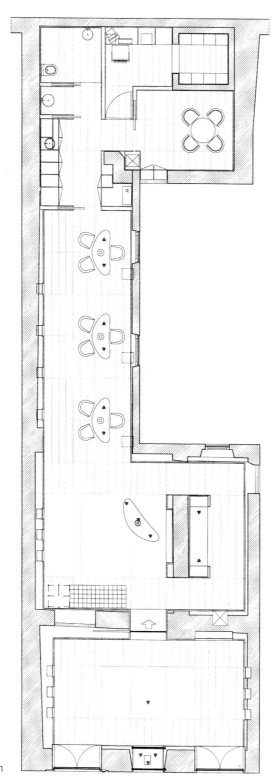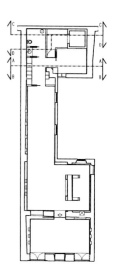

Floor plan

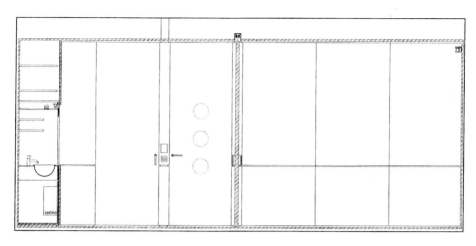

Cross section A-A

A sliding door located at the end of the customer service area is the access to the private area of the shop, which houses the services and space for offices, meetings and relaxation.

Creneau International Design
Pepe Jeans Flagship store
London, UK

A former art gallery was converted into the flagship boutique of the firm Pepe Jeans, located in Covent Garden, London. This scheme was highly conditioned by the restrictions imposed by the authorities, since it is a historical building and the conservation and modification of the exterior of the building were controlled by very strict regulations. Another factor, this time determined by the firm Pepe Jeans, was the shortage of time, since the opening of the store was planned for Christmas. In spite of the complications that accompanied the construction of the boutique, including a delay in the license exactly one week before the opening, it is a true example of originality.

The architects worked from the existing plans of the building. They carried out a study of the location and the surroundings and presented a series of sketches that showed how the historical aspects of the building could be respected. The objective was to create an elegant space in which to display the products of the Pepe Jeans brand. Starting from the initial client programme, more details were added and the proposal was refined. The cafeteria that had been planned at the rear of the second floor was moved to the front, and a small interior arcade was introduced inside the main door to be used as an evening access to the cafeteria. Most of the central structural elements were taken out of the sales area on the first floor.

The capacity to propose ideas and project them in space was an important part of the evolution of the design of this boutique. However, though they had an almost ideal backdrop, the architects faced the contradiction between the requirements of a modern space and the pressure of the conservation groups to maintain the appearance of the building intact. Having resolved the debate, they demolished the unwanted walls and removed the rubble. The interior furniture of the building –display units, shelves, tables and mirrors– are made of nickel.

Photographs: Frank Gielen

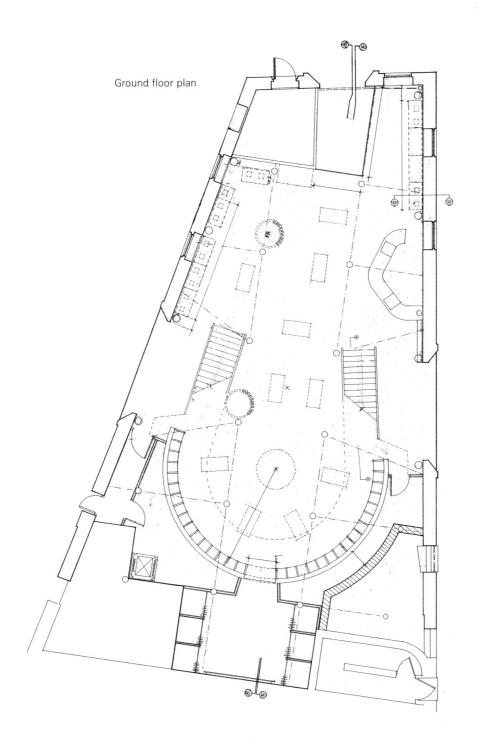

Ground floor plan

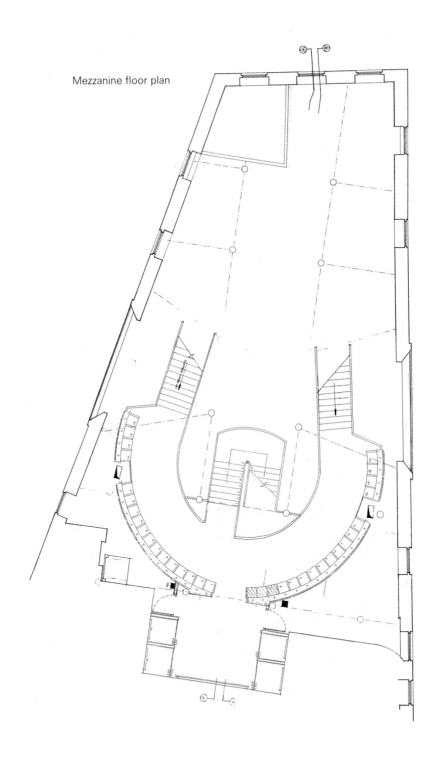

Mezzanine floor plan

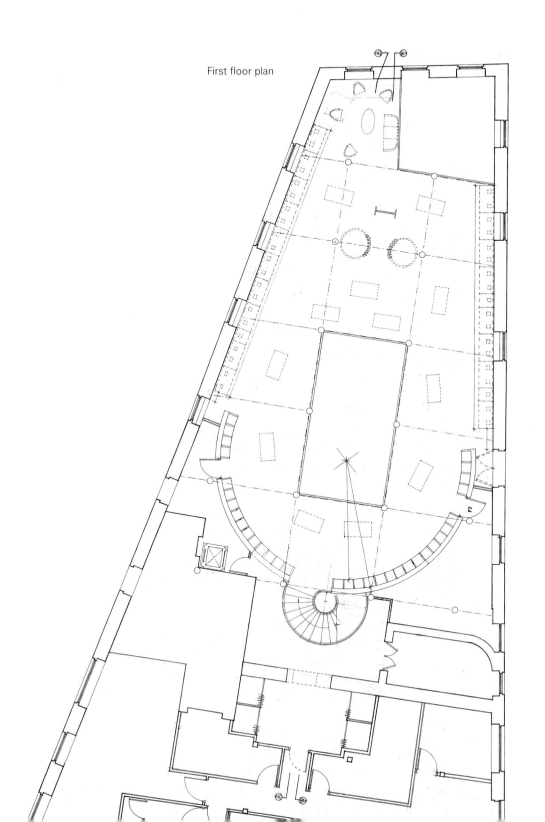

First floor plan

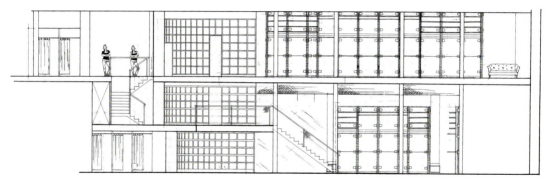

Section AA

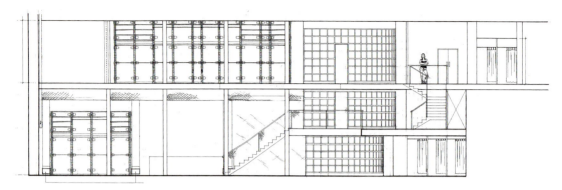

Section BB

Urquijo & Vázquez
Purificación García
Madrid & Barcelona, Spain

When undertaking the project for Purificación García's boutiques, the architects pursued above all simplicity of lines, with a unitary design combining aesthetics with functionalism. The space is stripped of all superfluous elements and is impregnated with a minimalist philosophy, using such simple and forceful materials as stone and wood. The void is the inspiration.

When approaching each project, a dialogue was established between the existing order and the new one that enters into contact with the first. The idea was to wrap the premises with a unitary skin that gives it meaning, to create a surrounding wall without touching anything, to create new forms without losing what is already there. It is more a case of cladding what already exists than creating something new, alien, cold. The store concept that was pursued is based on the search for a space that loses materiality with the light, with dematerialised walls, transformed into a whitish fog, creating cosy atmospheres in which the customers feel comfortable while planes and backgrounds of light attract their attention. Thus, the vision of the garments on display takes on greater importance.

The mirror reinforces the disappearance of the wall as a frontier: the image, bouncing from surface to surface, creates an infinite perspective that gives the impression that one is in a deceptively larger space. The predominant longitudinal dimension becomes the guideline of the project, using the linear axis as a spatial concept. The recovery of the original levels of the premises accentuates the creation of differentiated spaces that generate atmospheres. The walls move, they are given dynamism thanks to the light. A sequence of illuminated planes and different dark objects attracts with force and simplicity, so the clothes on display stand out against the purity of the illuminated white and contrast with the ebony wood. The lighting, which seems to emerge from the wall, creates almost magical spaces in which the walls and furniture fade away.

Photographs: Antonio Beas

Madrid

The pure, strict lines of the shop window are integrated harmoniously and delicately in the classicism of the facade. The store, occupying two floors, resembles a long circulation space flanked by the garments on display that attract the visitor's attention.

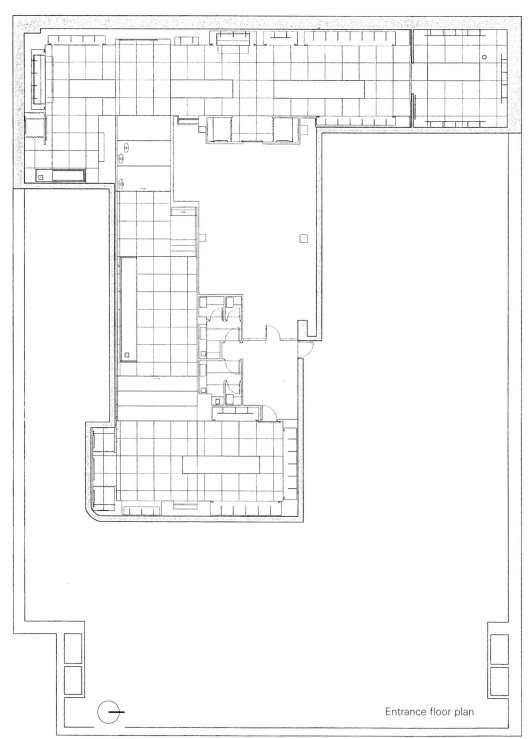
Entrance floor plan

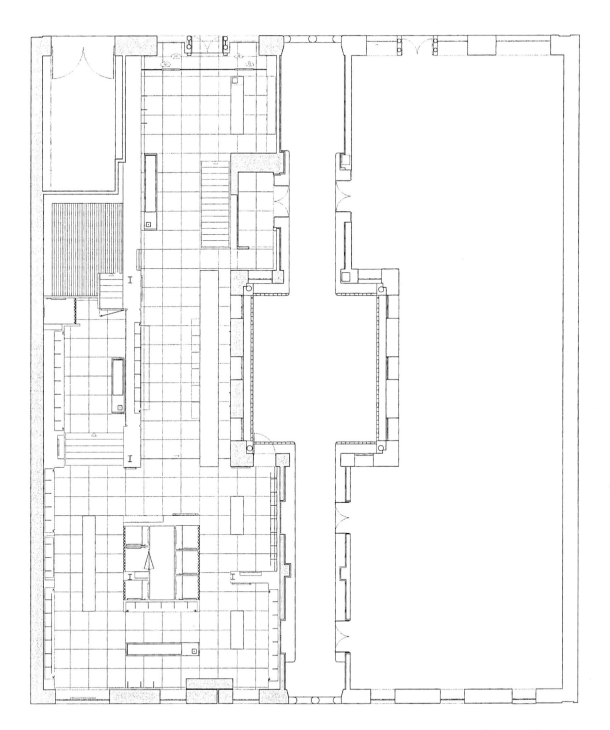

Basement floor plan

The chromatic uniformity that dominates in the boutique helps to enhance the products on display, and creates a sensation of immateriality, evoking an atmosphere in which the light plays a fundamental part in the definition of the spaces.

Barcelona

Purificación García's store in Barcelona, which occupies the ground floor of an impressive building in Passeig de Gràcia, maintains the constants of all the projects of the firm, adapting to the peculiarities of the location.

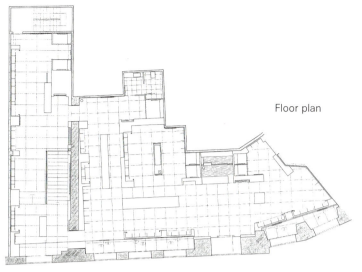

Floor plan

Venturi, Scott Brown & Associates
Exxon Gas Station for Disney World
Florida, USA

Venturi & Scott Brown have designed a prototypical gas station, a perfect and virtuoso interplay in which all the elements that normally define a gas station are combined, and the logo or name of the petrol company is a secondary element in the design of the generic roadside elements.

The solution that was adopted is that of a conventional canopy and large-scale-gas pump structure, which are connected to a self-service shop with large-scale graphics of the word EATS in a translucent frit applied to the inside of the glass curtain wall. Behind the gas station in the garden, characterised by an outer wall whose profile recalls the silhouette of the trees located just behind it.

Two optional solutions were adopted to provide a rapid view of the service area form any point of the road. They are both monumental solutions: 30-foot high, three-dimensional letters spelling "Gas" and a 75-foot high "Gas Pump" sign.

Photographs: Matt Wargo

View of the outer wall that separates and delimits the garden at the back of the service station. The silhouette of the wall matches that of the trees in the background.

General view of the service station, with the 22.5-meter-high column/sign rising above the service station.

The word "Eats" is inscribed on the inner glass wall in large letters made of porous translucent glass.
The interior of the shop is given a unique feel by the signs inscribed on the enclosing elements.

Jean Nouvel
Galeries Lafayette / Euralille Centre Comercial
Berlin, Germany / Euralille, France

In the design of this department store, the architect seeks to intercept passers-by in the street, on the pavement by prolonging the exterior public space of Friedrichstrasse. From the street the space of the ground floor is free, without any walls. The desmaterialization of the angle allows motorists and pedestrian to see the lights cones, the largest of which palpitates, shines, flash beams of light and colour.

The central nature of the department store in the block was also imposed. The spatial arrangement of the different levels is simple to read, as it allows everyone to know at all times where they are and where they are going. The two large cone-shaped mirrors in the central space are an object of fascination. Here, thanks to advertising campaigns, the messages and images run over the surfaces. A veritable question and a characterise the building by day, and even more so at night, the geometry and light create the architecture infinite variations linked to the time and the nature of the images that are programmed.

Located at the confluence of the Paris-London TGV line, the city of Lille is faced commissioned to design the large housing complex, a shopping centre, flanked by a row of houses, and a hotel in the east and five to towers in the south.

Concerned by coherence and differentiation, Jean Nouvel proposed unity of material, painted aluminium forming a theoretical grey background against which each element shows its specific signs and colours. The facades of the shopping centre and the towers, the lower and upper parts of the central roof, are punctuated with lights and coloured signs, which relate to the refreshing and mobile holograms within the airport vocabulary that is used in the centre. The long facade of the residential building offers a mosaic of vibrant colours under the changeable northern skies.

Photographs: Philippe Rualt

The building was designed to intercept the pedestrians, inviting them to enter the new public space that has been created inside the warehouses.

The transparent facade shows its signs in triangular haloes (that resonate with the cones of the interior) or rectangular ones (that are in proportion with the screen).

Ground floor plan

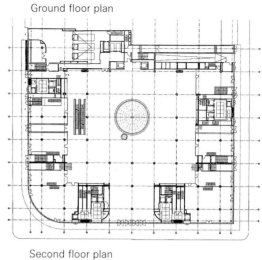

Third floor plan

Second floor plan

Fifth floor plan

Seventh floor plan

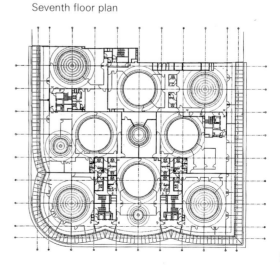

Sections

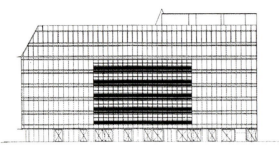
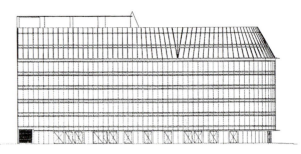
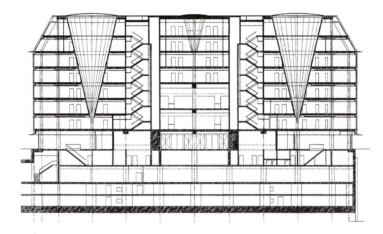

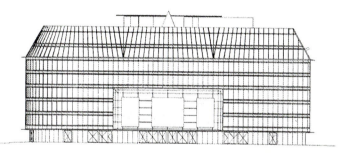
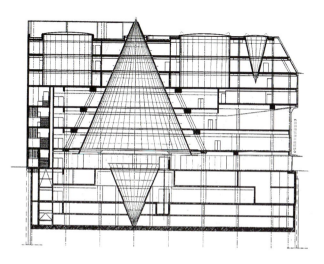

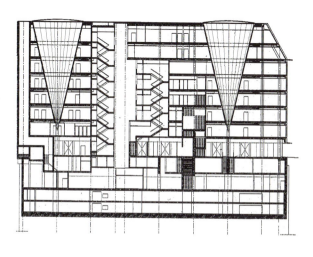

Euralille

In the interior of the Euralille Centre there is a predominance of airport vocabulary, with which a close relationship is established.
In the treatment of the facade the architect used painted aluminium that gives the building a dark grey background on which the colours of the signs stand out.

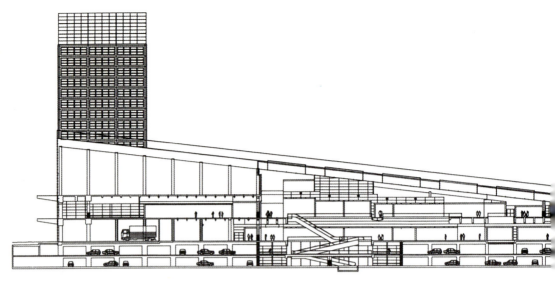

Longitudinal sections

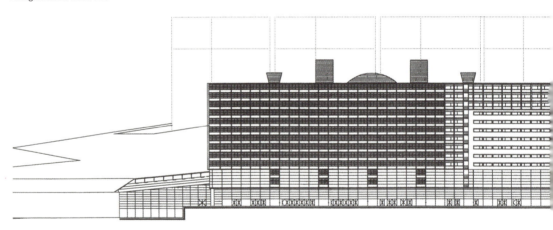

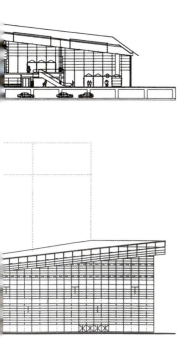

Sage Wimmer Coombe
Jancovic Plaza
New York City, USA

In the renovated space of the Janovic/Plaza paint store, light plays a fundamental role: it is an essential element for choosing a certain colour of paint, a wallpaper or a curtain. Colour is the other factor that defines the project. Following these guidelines, Sage Wimmer Coombe designed a shop in which illustrations and famous quotes about colour and the home entertain and inspire both professionals and amateurs.

The shop has been paved with white terrazzo tiles with inlays of small fragments of coloured glass. This type of floor unifies the space and provides a background on which the colours and more complex designs can coexist. The terrazzo is repeated in the tops of the tables distributed around the whole store. Large patches of paint unify the irregular design of the columns. Between the paint section and the home decoration section a space is devoted to colour selection. This environment of deliberately neutral tones has different types of light sources (incandescent lamps, fluorescent lamps, and different types of simulated natural light) so that the client can imagine the different possibilities of lighting that can be used in a house.

The oval moulding that presides over the wall conceals a lamp and illuminates the atmosphere in cavetto. Around this moulding is a quote from Paul Klee: "Painting well is no more than this: putting the right colour in the right place". In the section devoted to upholstery, tables with terrazzo tops allow the clients to choose in comfort. Six round lights illuminate this atmosphere surrounded by a soffit painted a deep purple and rich yellow on which illuminated frames display images of eye-catching rooms.

Photographs: Michael Moran

The first thing that surprises the visitor on entering the store is a mural with abstract images of cans of paint, tools, blinds and wallpapers in which two display units and three television monitors have been fitted. The shelves displaying the paints bear quotes from Alice Walker, Vincent van Gogh and William Blake.

1. Residential building lobby
2. Column
3. Store entry
4. Service entry
5. Cash desk
6. Window display
7. Display wall
8. Paint department
9. Colour selection room
10. Sliding window treatment display
11. Interior design centre
12. Emergency exit

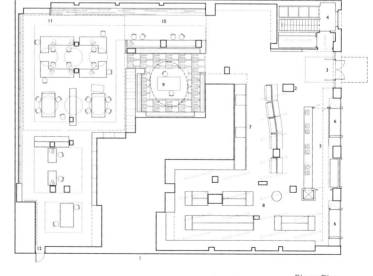

Floor Plan

Vincent van Duysen
Boutique Natan
Brussels, Belgium

The scheme for the Natan boutique, located in an old building in Brussels, consisted of creating a bright but private atmosphere. The space is articulated by means of white elements: the load-bearing walls, the pillars and the beams, the mezzanine that seems to float in space, the marble staircase contained in an angular balustrade and the light wall of the shop window parallel to the facade. Regardless of their abstraction, the minimalist white surfaces –some of them mobile– delimit the spaces where the customers, shielded from views from the street, can try on the garments while they enjoy the exterior views through a horizontal opening in the wall. The street thus becomes a shop window for the customers.

The display elements match the rest of the space in colour and materials, which gives uniformity to the whole and highlights the interplay of volumes and forms created between the vertical circulation space and the mezzanine.

The lighting systems, spotlights fitted into a hanging ceiling and perimeter lighting, help to multiply the brightness of the boutique. The hanging ceiling does not touch the wall, and, as if suspended in the air, it breaks for a moment the uniformity of the space. This arrangement forms part of the interplay of volumes and geometries of the scheme: lines abruptly cut off by others, juxtaposition and overlapping of bodies. The mezzanine highlights the vertical dimension of the space and creates an interplay of heights on the ground floor. Windows with black shutters on the outside and white ones on the inside lessen the impact of the entrance to the boutique and use the metaphor of colour to show the contrast between the hustle and bustle of the street and the clear peacefulness of this space. The interior is thus disconnected from the urban environment and the main role is given to the garments.

Photographs: Alberto Piovano

The combination of the existing curved elements of the building –the semi-circular arch of the windows and the access door– with the angularity of the new proposal helps to create a space whose layout does not follow an immediately obvious pattern.

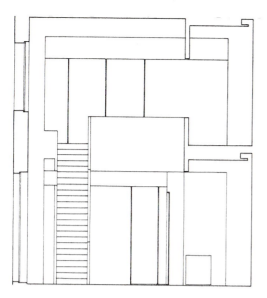 

Cross sections

Longitudinal section

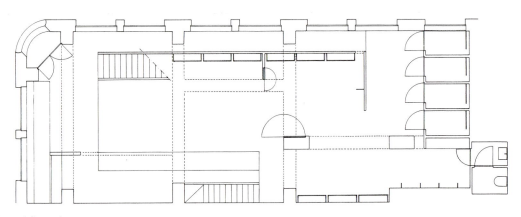

Ground floor plan

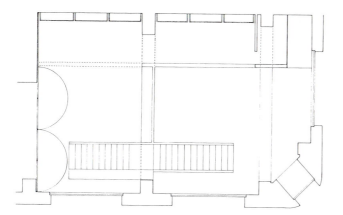

The location of the building that houses the boutique, at the corner of two streets, had a decisive influence on the design concept. The aim was to isolate the boutique by giving it a high degree of autonomy in order to prevent the urban environment from invading the interior space.

Frank F. Drewes
Sally & Sam
Warendorf & Wiedenbrük, Germany

The Sally & Sam stores in Warendoff and Wiedenbrük are the prototypes for a young clothing company. The design intention was to achieve an individual atmosphere within a tight budget. The solutions were simple, with handcrafted display units which were arranged in a strict orthogonal pattern.

The desired atmosphere was to be stylish and relaxed at the same time. The reduced formal language creates the architectonic look, whereas the simple and rough materials are expected to age gracefully.

The basic equipment of each store are the display units which are specified for each location individually. Few architectural manipulations are designed particularly in order to correspond to the uniqueness of each store. Such elements are the dressing rooms, the stairs in Warendorf and the dropped ceiling in Wiedenbrük.

The main intention of the Sally & Sam stores is to entertain the customers with the atmosphere and to present the merchandise as part of the unique whole.

Photographs: Christian Ritchers

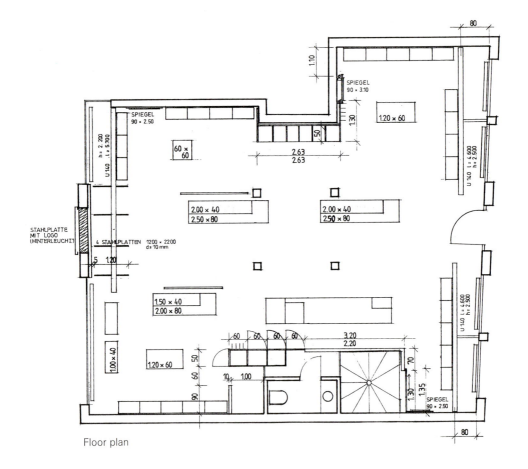

Floor plan

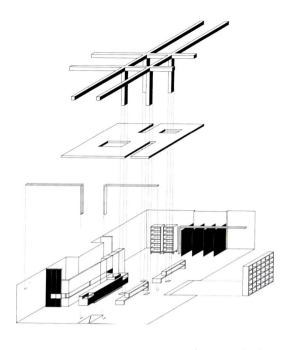

Axonometric view

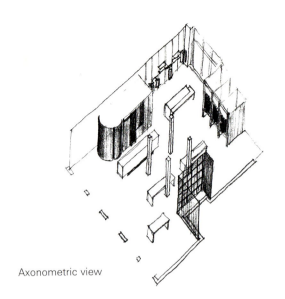

Axonometric view

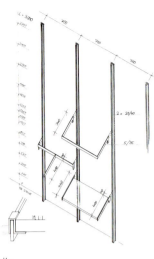

Construction details

The changing rooms, with their basic, rudimentary construction of unfinished beams and metal panels, echo the geometric layout of the store and the philosophy of the brand: simplicity and authenticity.

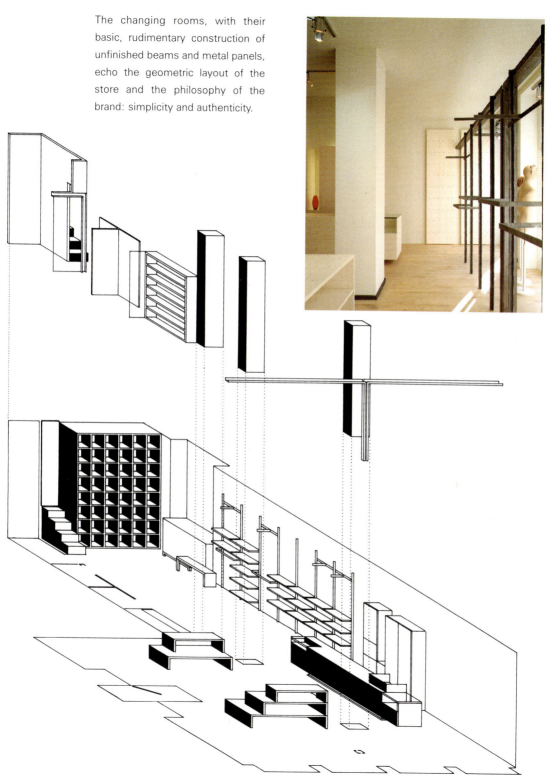

The fixtures are of raw materials, such as wood and metal, that will be enriched through use. The display elements are primarily functional. Their main roles are acting as separations between the different areas of the shop and showcasing the clothes.

Javier Mozas
Chemist's in calle Postas
Vitoria-Gasteiz, Spain

The facade of this scheme breaks with the traditional style of access to this type of establishment. The interior space is separated from the exterior by means of two stainless steel frames with glass panels. One of them is sliding and bears a translucent sign that forms part of the shop window when the shop is open and covers beechwood panelling when it is closed. The position of the sign thus indicates whether the chemist's is open or closed.

In order to create a large space, interior subdivision was avoided. The elements contained in this single space are low and mobile. The floor and ceiling are continuous and in warm colours. The ceiling is located at the highest point allowed by the beams of the building and the fitted lighting creates a horizontal effect on its surface. The warehouse and the office, located on the mezzanine, are integrated visually in the main space because there are no opaque walls. The office is separated from the back room by glass panels of different degrees of transparency.

The two walls that close the premises lengthways set into play the concepts of opacity and transparency. The right wall is made of glass and contains the access door to the mezzanine. This door reproduces the fantastic sensation of going through a mirror. The upper part of this glass wall is translucent and serves as a light diffuser, like a large flat lamp that serves as a separation. In contrast, the left wall is opaque and has the warm and tactile texture of wood; without transparencies or holes it forms an impenetrable physical limit.

Photographs: *a+t* / César San Millán

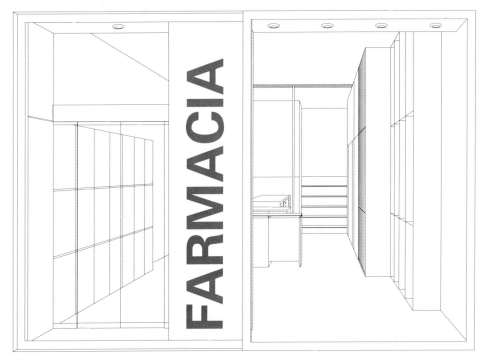

Elevation of the access

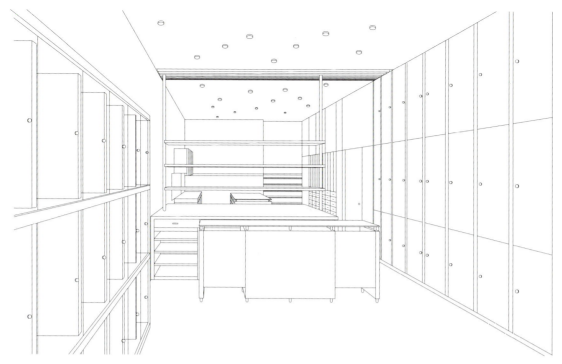

Perspective of the access

To prevent the overlapping of the sliding frame and the window from creating unwanted reflections, a special glass with an anti-reflective treatment was used.

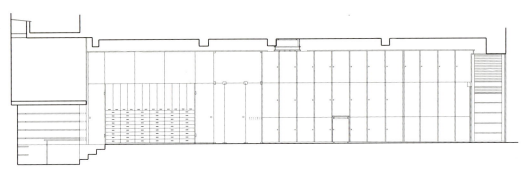

Transparent section

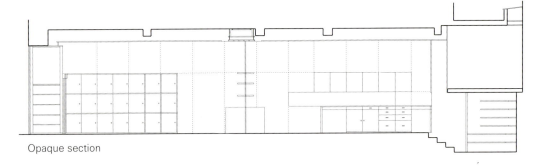

Opaque section

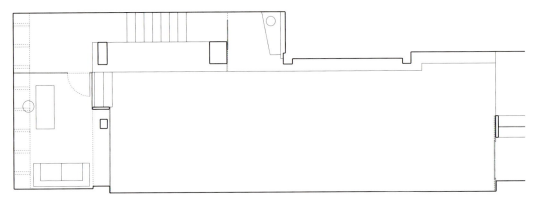

Upper floor plan

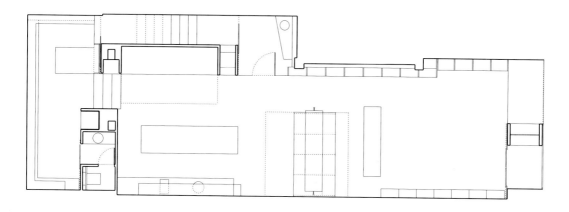

Ground floor plan

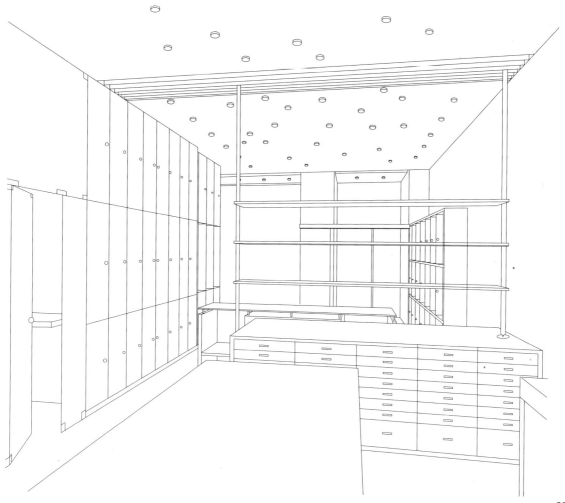

Peter Marino Assoc. Architects
Louis Vuitton
Paris, France

This project is the introductory boutique for Louis Vuitton's presentation of Ready to Wear, a natural compliment to their classic trunk and leather goods lines.

A new glass and bronze facade sits within an important 1930s Art Deco building, inviting visitors to enter from a dynamic corner of the Champs Élysées. They are welcomed into a tall rotunda lined with wood and polished plaster. Spaces flow through this hinge, creating an environment of glamorous luxury.

A large void surrounded by glass, bronze and exotic wood marquetry allows for views from the ground floor into the spacious lower level. Here another rotunda echoes the spatial experience of upstairs. Warm wood floors and taupe and ecru wool area rugs continue throughout.

A separate entrance to the Men's Store is located along Avenue Georges V, allowing shoppers to enter rooms of striated plaster and marquetry lined walls. Here an open wood and bronze stair surrounds a glass elevator.

Photographs: David Cardelús

Facade Avenue George V

Facade Champs-Élysées

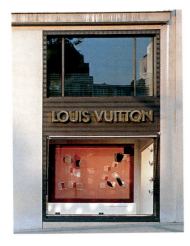

The windows of Louis Vuitton's new store are integrated discreetly into the building. The main facade, at the corner of Avenue George V and the Champs Élysées, houses the entrance to the women's boutique. The entrance to the men's boutique is on Avenue George V.

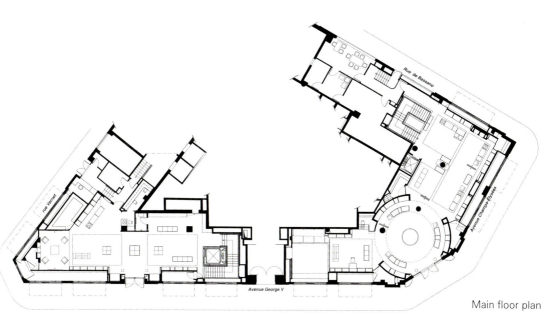

Main floor plan

The distribution of the different environments inside the boutique reflects the desire to present the products in a relaxed and sober atmosphere. The rotundas of the access floor and the lower level articulate the different environments and have armchairs that can be used for relaxing and communication.